Under the Rust Belt

PAUL MARTIN SERIES ON
LEADERSHIP AND INNOVATION

Paul Martin Series on Leadership and Innovation

Thomas Bacher, Editor, *Under the Rust Belt: Revealing Innovation in Northeast Ohio*

Under the Rust Belt

Revealing Innovation in Northeast Ohio

Thomas Bacher, Editor

Carol Slatter, Assistant Editor

With the assistance of Caitlyn Caldwell,
Matt Margo, Katelyn Mertz, and Emily Tara

The University of Akron Press
Akron, Ohio

19 18 17 16 15 5 4 3 2 1

ISBN: 978-1-937378-21-9 (paperback)

LIBRARY OF CONGRESS CATALOGING-IN-PUBLICATION DATA
Under the rust belt : revealing innovation in Northeast Ohio / edited by Thomas Bacher.
pages cm. — (Paul Martin series on leadership and innovation)
Includes bibliographical references and index.
ISBN 978-1-937378-21-9 (pbk. : alk. paper)
1. Technological innovations—Economic aspects—Ohio. 2. Manufacturing industries—Technological innovations—Ohio. 3. Entrepreneurship—Ohio. 4. Ohio—Economic conditions. I. Bacher, Thomas.
HC107.O323T485 2015
338.9771'3—dc23

2014044269

∞ The paper used in this publication meets the minimum requirements of ANSI/NISO z39.48–1992 (Permanence of Paper).

Cover Design and Illustration: Samantha Pasa

Under the Rust Belt was designed and typeset in Caslon with Helvetica Neue display by Amy Freels with assistance from Samantha Pasa, and printed on sixty-pound natural and bound by Bookmasters of Ashland, Ohio.

For Paul Martin

Contents

Part II Innovators at Work: Conversations

Part III Educating Future Innovators

Appendix

Preface
Entrepreneurship

Deborah D. Hoover

For some time now, a robust interest in entrepreneurship has been growing at the youth, collegiate, and adult levels in Northeast Ohio. At the youth level, thousands of students in schools and youth groups across the region participate each year in programs such as Camp Invention or Lemonade Day, two of the country's preeminent innovation and entrepreneurship programs for elementary school children. Lemonade Day allows them to explore entrepreneurship through the timeless first commercial experience for most young people—starting and running a lemonade stand—while Camp Invention utilizes STEM and entrepreneurship curricula that offer students the opportunity to think critically, problem solve, and work in a team. Middle and high school students are able to join in academic programs offered at their respective schools as well as participate in nationally renowned free enterprise programs such as Junior Achievement.

At the adult level, the philanthropic collaborative, the Fund for Our Economic Future, paved the way over the last decade for entrepreneurial support organizations such as BioEnterprise, NorTech, and JumpStart to help aspiring entrepreneurs boost their innovations and ventures to the next level and thus positively impact the Northeast Ohio economy. For our region, this transition from Rust Belt to a growing, vibrant economy will not be sustainable without the dedication and perseverance of young entrepreneurs.

Interest is accelerating among the throngs of college students eager to learn about the entrepreneurial mind-set and even to start their own business venture. Every year, thousands enroll in courses, take part in idea competitions or other cocurricular activities, and participate in internship programs. Incredibly, almost every college or university in Northeast Ohio, from large state universities to small liberal arts colleges, is offering some type of entrepreneurship program. Many of the area's collegiate institutions have also come together to form the Entrepreneurship Education Consortium—its programs for young entrepreneurs have been nationally recognized by the United States Association for Small Business and Entrepreneurship (USASBE).

Five colleges (Baldwin Wallace University, Hiram College, Lake Erie College, Oberlin College, and the College of Wooster) participated in the funding partnership begun by The Burton D. Morgan Foundation and the Ewing Marion Kauffman Foundation seven years ago, the Northeast Ohio Collegiate Entrepreneurship Program (NEOCEP). NEOCEP inspired young people, opening the door of entrepreneurship to thousands of students at small colleges eager to try their hand at running a fledgling business. At Oberlin College, for example, recent graduates compete to land yearlong fellowships to start their own ventures. Several ventures begun at the outset of the program have seen great success, including Inkren, a technology company that developed software to help students learn Chinese and Japanese characters and received follow-on support from the Innovation Fund of Lorain County Community College. Students at the College of Wooster (COW) have worked as entrepreneurship interns in a variety of capacities at ABS Materials, a company launched by a COW chemistry professor, leading to full-time positions.

Blackstone LaunchPad, a collaboration between The Blackstone Charitable Foundation of New York and the Morgan Foundation, will allow over seventy-two thousand students in Northeast Ohio to have the opportunity to start their own business. Baldwin Wallace University, Kent State University, Case Western Reserve University, and Lorain County Community College will be participating in this new initiative based on a very successful cocurricular program started at the University of Miami. Students will receive one-on-one counseling with trained consultants at their colleges and many benefits later from venture coaching by volunteer professionals. These programs, groups, and institutions together form an extensive collegiate entrepreneurial ecosystem that collectively coordinates business plan competitions, internship experiences, and an immersion week providing rich experiential opportunities for the region's students. We are also fortunate to have a number of resources available to assist student entrepreneurs as they transition from collegiate entrepreneurship programs to business accelerators and incubators such as MAGNET and Shaker LaunchHouse.

The Burton D. Morgan Foundation has been supporting young entrepreneurs in our region for several decades. This would not be possible, of course, without the foresight Mr. Morgan had in creating the foundation that bears his name and recognizing the need for the region to support aspiring entrepreneurs. The trustees of the foundation believe its definition of entrepreneurship, "the process of identifying and developing a new economic venture or solution that adds value, embodies innovation and creativity, and involves risk to its initiators," clearly conveys what future entrepreneurs might be inspired to achieve through their work. Similarly, our mission is straightforward and simple: "To strengthen the free enterprise system by investing in organizations and institutions that foster the entrepreneurial spirit." This mission crystallizes our vision to perpetuate a "free enterprise society of economically independent citizens who support the entrepreneurial spirit and contribute to the improvement of their communities."

Ultimately, we hope the stories shared in this book will inspire others to get involved in the movement to reinvent our economy. Through the mentorship of young people, we will strengthen our nation's natural inclination to create and grow innovative ventures and to excel in entrepreneurial thinking. The introduction of the entrepreneurial mind-set to young people and the creation of enticing pathways help to guide students to pursue increasingly challenging opportunities and goals. After all, entrepreneurial success is at the very roots of our great nation and is key to ensuring the health and vitality of our economic future. Our collective work in Northeast Ohio serves as a laboratory for reimagining a national identity based on capturing the verve of the entrepreneur and translating innovative ideas from concept to reality.

Introduction

Thomas Bacher

As a child growing up in a blue-collar neighborhood of Cleveland, I have memories of a three-shift transmission manufacturing plant bellowing out smoke from its stacks at the end of Stumph Road. Machine shops and other industries dotted the area around the plant employing thousands of workers. Neighborhoods grew, schools were filled, and restaurants were packed for all-you-could-eat fish fries during the Lenten season.

The story of the decline in the area's manufacturing prominence has been well told. Population and local tax revenue went elsewhere. The Rust Belt was born.

This particular volume is not meant to provide complete answers for the area's rebirth. Those answers are as varied as the many ethnic populations in greater Cleveland and Northeast Ohio. Zeal and innovation, however, are traits that can become dynamic forces in a new Northeast Ohio, one in which start-ups can spur economic growth.

This collection was several years in the making. At the start, the idea was to ask area innovators the following questions:

- Since innovation depends on ideas, how do you go about generating new ideas? Do you use a specific process?

- As an entrepreneur, what motivated you to work in the specific field you chose?
- How does the concept of "risk" play a part in your decision-making process?
- Did you fail before you succeeded?
- In what respects were you least prepared and in what respects most prepared for your venture?
- To what extent was your venture a technology, product, or service initially seeking a market, or a market seeking a solution or provider?
- What were the major barriers you encountered and how did you overcome them?
- Did your effort require outside capital, and if so, what was your experience in obtaining such financing?
- Did any specific areas of your education play a part in how you decided to approach your venture?
- Do you think aspects of your background or upbringing, outside of education, played a large role in your entrepreneurial activity?
- Some economists have said that for sustained growth, a supply of entrepreneurs needs to be developed. How can this be done?
- What was and is your primary motivation as a pioneer in your field?
- How can the Northeast Ohio region better support innovation and entrepreneurship?
- What would you tell an aspiring innovator?

The study is not exhaustive and should be viewed as a starting point to better understand Northeast Ohio and what the area can offer to innovators and entrepreneurs. During the late 1800s and early 1900s, settlers and pioneers were starting business in what was then known as the Western Reserve. The first rubber cord bicycle tire was manufactured in Akron in 1892 and the first nonskid automobile tire was patented in Akron in 1914. The first electric arc lights were installed in Cleveland in 1879 and first electric traffic signal was installed at the corner of Euclid Avenue and East 105th Street in 1914. In the early 1880s, a group of forward-thinking Youngstownians set up the Humanitarian Invention Association to develop the inventive genius of the area. Hopefully, Northeast Ohio can once again become a stimulating environment for new entrepreneurs and new technologies.

Part I

Northeast Ohio, Culture, and Economic Climate

Cleveland and the Region

A Planning Perspective, 2000–2014

Norman Krumholz and Kathryn Wertheim Hexter

The turn of the twenty-first century saw progress on several fronts. The city's first female mayor, Jane Campbell (2002–2006), hoped to use her control of the long-neglected public school system to reform and improve its operations. This concern was echoed by her successor, Frank Jackson, the city's third African American mayor who was first elected in 2006 and remained mayor in 2014. The city prepared and adopted a lakefront plan, with new beaches, miles of bike trails, marinas, and new neighborhoods. The business community sought to build a new convention center to replace an outmoded one. The Greater Cleveland Regional Transit Authority (RTA) began planning a bus rapid transit line along Euclid Avenue from downtown to University Circle, Cleveland's commercial spine. Planners hoped to control regional sprawl which they believed was sucking population, jobs, and investment out of the core city. Neighborhood revitalization was beginning to achieve significant progress, led by a group of neighborhood-based community development corporations, the Cleveland Housing Network, and several intermediaries that had become national models.

Over the decade, the city achieved many of its objectives. RTA completed the rebuilding of Euclid Avenue and its new bus rapid transit system, a $200 million project largely financed by the federal government. For the first time in decades, private development began to flow back toward Euclid Avenue. Much of that development focused on a building boom in University Circle, home of Case Western Reserve University, the city's major museums, the Cleveland Orchestra, and two major hospitals. The Cleveland Clinic became one of Ohio's largest hospitals and employers. University Circle continued to be one of the region's most important employment centers along with downtown. A new $450 million convention center, funded by a countywide sales tax on the mall opened in June 2013, creating anticipation for more conventions and more tourists.[1] The complex features a Global Center for Health Innovation which hopes to attract medical groups and take advantage of Cleveland's prominent health care sector. Cuyahoga County broke ground in 2014 for a new, publicly financed convention hotel adjacent to the center. Following approval in a statewide 2008 election, a new casino, the first in Cleveland's history, opened in an extensively remodeled department store on Public Square. City, county and state tax revenue generated by the casino was less than promised but helped to partially offset severe budget cuts at the federal and state level.

A major upheaval changed the form of government of Cuyahoga County. County residents, who had been governed by three county commissioners for close to two hundred years, overwhelmingly voted in 2009 to end the commissioner form and replace it with an elected county executive and a county council. This followed revelations of extensive corruption throughout the commissioner system which ended with one commissioner, other officials, and developers in jail. Presumably, the new government structure will be more honest, representative, and transparent than the old.

Small steps were taken toward a more regional approach to planning and economic development. Several inner suburbs began facing the problems that had challenged Cleveland for many years: population out-migration, rising levels of poverty, and inadequate local tax revenues. In response, the sixteen inner suburbs of Cleveland formed the First Suburbs Consortium in 1997. Its purpose was to counteract sprawl in the metropolitan region and to lobby and advocate for changes in state policies to provide more assistance to older suburbs.[2] Other attempts to facilitate cooperative regional decision making include: the Fund for Our Economic Future, a regional effort to stimulate economic growth and retain jobs, and the Northeast Ohio Sustainable Communities Consortium, a group of thirty-two organizations from across twelve counties that have come together to encourage regional land use planning. A federal grant provided the incentive for this unprecedented planning effort. The Northeast Ohio Areawide Coordinating Agency (NOACA) continues to serve as the five-county agency for transportation planning as it has for the past forty years.

In 2010, downtown Cleveland realized the first signs of population growth in decades. From 1990 to 2010 the downtown population grew 96 percent from 4,561 residents to 9,098 residents. Furthermore, residential occupancy tended to remain at just over 95 percent. Additionally encouraging, this population seems to be weighted with highly educated young adults in the 22–34 age range. These residents are more likely to be positioned well in the new knowledge-based economy of the era. A few of Cleveland's other neighborhoods, including Ohio City, Tremont, and Detroit Shoreway are also experiencing a net in-migration of 25–34 age range. This is important to note considering that the city as a whole is still losing residents.[3] This may indicate that downtown, Ohio City, and Tremont's efforts to brand themselves as great places for young professionals to live have been successful. Even more encouraging, between 2000 and 2012, the Cleveland metro area logged a net gain of about sixty thousand people 25 and over with a college degree while losing a net of seventy thousand of those without a bachelor's degree. Half emigrated from out of state.[4] The Downtown Alliance and the Community Development Corporations (CDCs) of Ohio City and Tremont emphasized assets like historic housing stock, urban excitement, and trendy retail.

These signs of optimism and progress must be tempered, however, by the continuing reality of the city's many challenges. Cleveland again suffered a significant population loss during the 2000–2010 decade, losing 17 percent. The number of residents fell from 478,000 to 396,000, making the city's population almost equivalent to its 1900 count. During this decade suburban Cuyahoga County also lost population, losing 2.3 percent. Future population projections for the entire Cleveland-Elyria-Mentor region were discouraging, forecasting a loss of 4.5 percent over the next thirty years while other regions in the US were projected to grow by up to 35 percent.[5]

Cleveland's population remains highly segregated and a majority of its residents continue to be members of minority groups. Based on a calculation of dissimilarity index scores, Cleveland's metropolitan area ranks fifth nationally in racial segregation amongst metropolitan areas of over five hundred thousand population with a score of 74.14.[6] Additionally concerning, Cleveland regularly ranks behind Detroit in the percentage of its population living in poverty. In 1999, Cleveland's poverty rate was 26.27 percent, with child poverty reaching 37.97 percent. In comparison, Cuyahoga County as a whole had a poverty rate of only 13.13 percent and a child poverty rate of 19.67 percent. Of 179,372 county residents living below the poverty line, 122,479 were Cleveland residents, accounting for 68.28 percent of all persons living below the poverty line in the county.

The Brookings Institution found that across the nation between 1990 and 2000 the number of people living in high poverty neighborhoods, defined as having poverty rates above 40 percent, declined by 24 percent. It appears that Cleveland also experienced this slightly optimistic deconcentration of poverty. In 1989, 73 of Cleveland's 197 census tracts had high concentrations of poverty, roughly 37 percent.[7] By 1999, only 49 census tracts of 225 had highly concentrated poverty, or roughly 22 percent.[8]

The Cuyahoga Metropolitan Housing Authority (CMHA), which in 1990 owned and operated more than twelve thousand housing units for the very poor, has demolished about three thousand of the most dilapidated units. Almost all of those units were in the city of Cleveland since suburban communities had declined to cooperate in the acceptance of public housing. Instead of replacing the units demolished with new, permanent units, CMHA now administers about fourteen thousand housing choice vouchers in Cuyahoga County which are being used to rent private housing anywhere in the city or the suburbs. Since the vouchers are used in the private market, no municipal agreement is needed. Of the total number of vouchers, about 6,700 are being used in Cleveland and about 4,700 are being used in just five suburbs on the near eastside.[9]

Development in the greater Cleveland region had been based on a growth strategy that was seriously flawed. The strategy consisted of five elements: (1) the widespread ownership of detached, single-family housing spreading indefinitely outward from the center city; (2) the ownership and use of private automobiles; (3) building destinations for working and shopping at low densities with plenty of free parking; (4) housing the poor mostly through trickle-down housing and thus concentrating them into backwater neighborhoods near the urban core; (5) supporting the above with highly fragmented and virtually autonomous governmental structures. Little has been done since 1999 to alter that strategy: out-migration continues in the region, new development spawns congestion in certain growth areas followed by demands for new road and sewer taxes, the poor, especially the minority poor, continue to be isolated in the city and abutting suburbs, and multiple, small, autonomous governments continue to preside over the region. Despite efforts to craft regional solutions, decision making in the region continues to be fragmented with each of the fifty-eight communities in Cuyahoga County competing for new investment, growth, and tax rateables.

Cleveland was hit hard by the collapse of the housing and financial markets which began in 2007. It engulfed many of the city's neighborhoods and left many thousands of vacant, abandoned, and foreclosed houses in its wake. The Slavic Village neighborhood (up until then, one of Cleveland's most successfully revitalized neighborhoods) became a national example of the devastating impact of subprime lending experienced by urban neighborhoods.[10] By 2013, Cleveland had some sixteen thousand vacant and abandoned houses, about half of which will be candidates for demolition due to their dilapidated condition. The magnitude of demolitions is far beyond the ability of the city to finance on its own. This confronts the city with another problem: what to do with the vacant land for which there is no apparent reuse? Fortunately, Cuyahoga County established a Land Bank in 2009 which is able to acquire tax delinquent and foreclosed properties and also to demolish and rehabilitate them and support redevelopment. Using the federal government's Neighborhood Stabilization Program and other resources, the Land Bank (through June, 2012) acquired about seventeen hundred properties and demolished about one thousand.[11] The city also fought back against irresponsible lenders and mortgage brokers in an effort to reduce the rate of foreclosures, halt the marketing of substandard housing to speculators, and begin the long-term process of rebuilding ravaged neighborhoods. Imaginative efforts have begun to convert vacant land to such uses as urban agriculture and farms, parks, and storm-water management systems.[12] It seems clear that the Cleveland of the future will have a smaller population and have much more green space than the Cleveland of the past.

Reform of the public school system also was vexing. Superintendents or CEOs, appointed by the mayor to improve the system, came and went while enrollment and reputation of the system continued to decline. Many schools were closed and demolished or rehabilitated even as some new schools were built with the support from the state of Ohio. As teachers and their unions were blamed for the poor performance of their students, the public system lost support and a growing number of private and public-private charter schools emerged. The mayor and school leaders, who had previously opposed charter schools, now announced their support. In 2012, the state legislature passed into law the Cleveland Plan for Transforming Schools which promised to improve student performance and graduation rates by rigorous testing, closing failing schools, and attacking teachers' seniority rules. A substantial increase in Cleveland's property tax rate was necessary to implement the Plan for Transforming Schools. In November 2012, voters passed a 15 mill tax levy for the Cleveland schools, the first operating levy passed since 1996. While urging the city's voters to pass the tax, the state also cut its financial contribution to the Cleveland school system. However, in 2013, the state budget included a $6 million earmark for the Cleveland schools to support the Cleveland Plan. This earmark gives Cleveland additional money beyond the traditional state funding for all school districts. Without the money, Cleveland would have been one of about two hundred districts statewide slated to see no increase in state funding over the next two years.

In terms of disparities in incomes, the trends are concerning. The median household income for whites in Cuyahoga County was $48,768 in 2000 according to the US Census. Yet, median household income for black residents was only $31,088. The American Community Survey from 2005–2009 showed similar income disparities, with whites having a median household income of $55,808 and blacks having a median household income of $35,544.[13] It is clear that problems persist with respect to income disparities, housing, and residential segregation. The city needs to tackle problems before officials become too optimistic about progress being made.

In 1999, the authors recommended[14] that Cleveland and its region adopt as top priorities three objectives: (1) reduce racial segregation in housing; (2) reform and improve the public education system; (3) establish a system of regional governance to address regional issues and control growth. By 2012, it was clear that neither the city nor the region were addressing the first priority. Racial segregation in the city and the inner-ring suburbs continued to be high. There were no proactive activities such as efforts to pass inclusionary zoning that would mandate a portion of affordable housing in all new developments of scale. Nor were there any efforts to rigorously enforce existing fair housing legislation. Rather than distributing capital improvements to the city's neighborhoods, the city and county administrations are "doubling down" on downtown with plans for a new $270 million, publicly funded convention center hotel, a new $75 million county administration building, and a $30 million revamp of Public Square.

Reform of the public education system was another matter; Cleveland was clearly addressing school reform through the Cleveland Plan for Transforming Schools. It is still too early to imagine the outcome of this effort, but with passage of the levy, there is no doubt that the city is trying hard for improvement. By 2014, however, Cleveland students continued to lag on state achievement tests. On the questions of regional efforts to control growth, the efforts made thus far have been weak. NOACA, the five-county area wide planning agency, confines its activities to transportation and some environmental issues, the First Suburbs Consortium has not been successful in lobbying the state to refocus its spending priorities toward older suburbs, and other agencies dealing with regional challenges are new and lack broad constituencies.

As with former industrial cities in the Rust Belt, this picture of Cleveland since 2000 presents a mix of persistent economic and social problems, along with efforts not only to cope but to transform the city in the face of seemingly intractable obstacles. As with many other cities, Cleveland can point to successes and failures as it attempts to identify a new role for its future.

This chapter originally appeared in the book, *The New American City Faces its Regional Future*, edited by David C. Sweet, Kathryn Wertheim Hexter, and David Beach and published by Ohio University Press, 1999. It has been updated by the authors.

Population and Social Characteristics

Stavros T. Constantinou

Population

In 2010, Northeast Ohio, a seventeen-county region, encompassed slightly less than 20 percent of the area of the state and approximately 37 percent of its population. As defined here it comprised seventeen counties in the northeastern part of the state of Ohio with a total population of 4,243,338 people. A comparison of the 2010 population for Northeast Ohio to the population for 2000 revealed a population loss of 2.5 percent. The majority of the region's population resided in cities and townships with more than 5,000 people (Fig. 1). In recently released estimates (June 2012) of the resident population for minor civil divisions in Ohio for the period April 1, 2011 to July 1, 2011, eight cities had an estimated population in excess of 50,000. Cleveland ranked first with 393,806 people, followed by Akron with 198,402, Parma with 80,968, Canton with 72,919, Youngstown with 66,560, Lorain with 64,152, Elyria with 54,581, and Lakewood with 51,724.

The seventeen-county area in Northeast Ohio is densely populated (Fig. 2). Three counties had population densities in excess of 1,000 persons per square mile: Cuyahoga, Summit, and Lake. In 2010, Cuyahoga County had an extremely high population density,

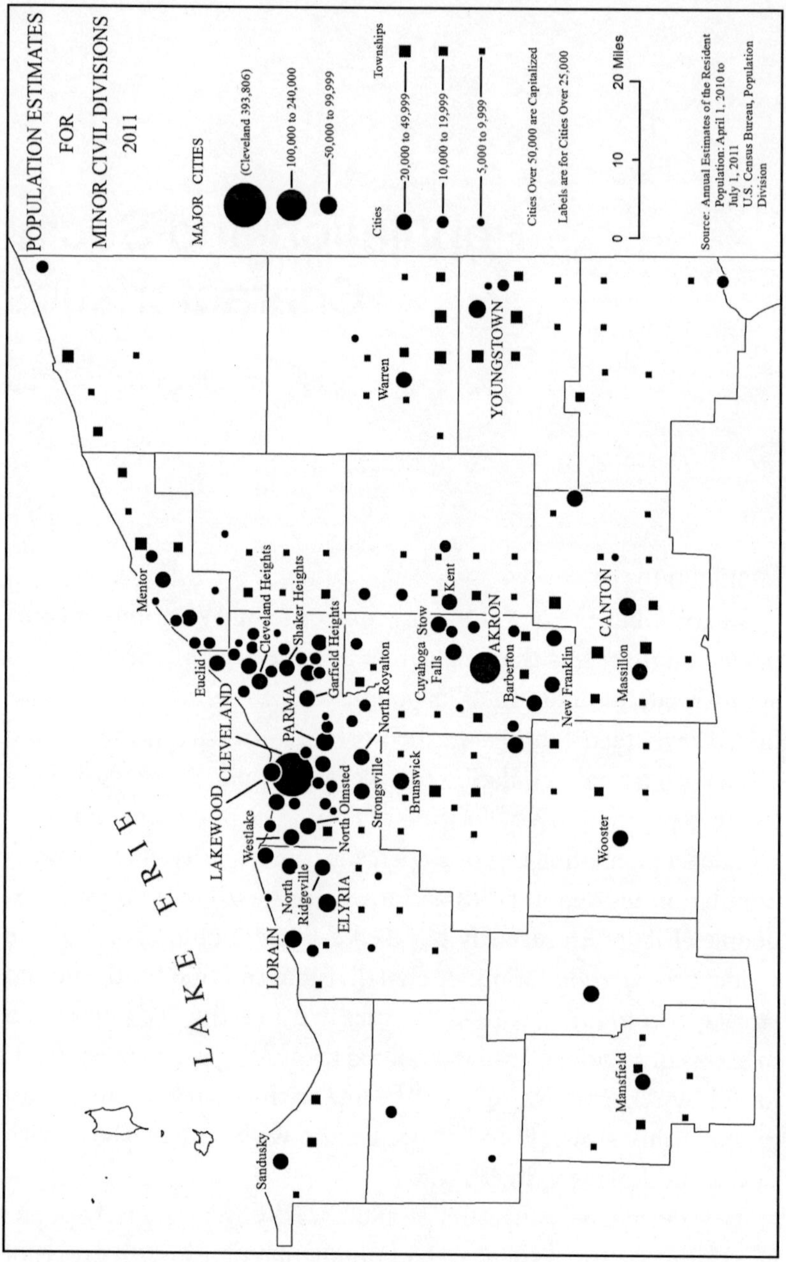

Figure 1. Populations of cities and townships over 5, 000.

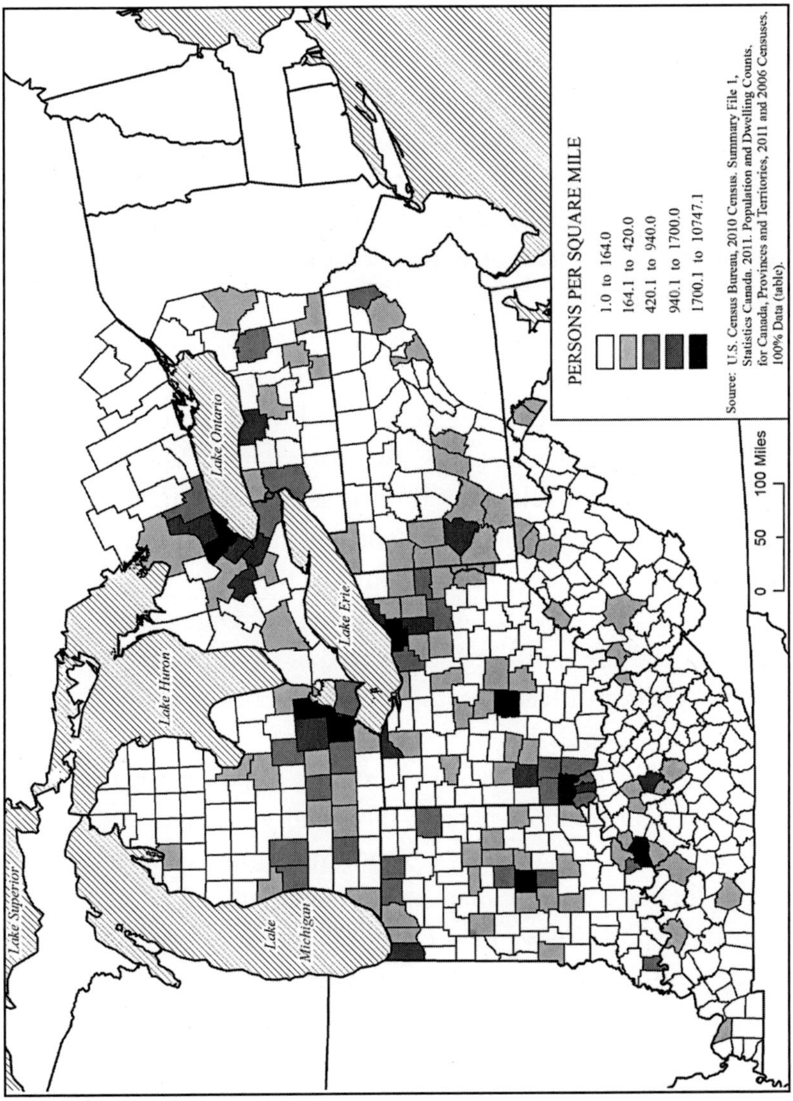

Figure 2. Population density.

an average of 2,800 persons per square mile (1,700.1 to 10,747.1 persons per square mile). In addition to Cuyahoga County, high population densities are found in Summit County with an average of 1,312.6 persons per square mile (940.1 to 1700 persons per square mile). Three counties—Huron, Ashland, and Ashtabula—had the lowest population densities in Northeast Ohio (1.0 to 164.0 persons per square mile). Their population densities were an average of 121.3, 125.6, and 144.6, respectively.

There is a linear distribution of cities and townships following the shoreline of Lake Erie and is particularly dense in Cuyahoga County. This urban cluster extends southwards into Summit and Stark counties, with a smaller concentration in Mahoning and Trumbull counties. Taken together, these cities and townships form the outlines of an emerging megalopolis along the Lake Erie region.

Ashland is the most rural county in the region, followed by Huron and Ashtabula. The eastern portions of Geauga and Portage counties, and the southwestern section of Medina county, which have not yet been affected by the spillover from Cuyahoga County, also have low population concentrations.

The mobility of population in Northeast Ohio appears to comply with three types of movement: (1) intracounty migrants, people who move only short distances; (2) intrastate migrants, people who move within the state; and (3) interstate and international migrants.

In general, the movement of population in Northeast Ohio is largely confined within the same county and, therefore, the migrants move a short distance (Fig. 3).

Population change in Northeast Ohio during the census years 1960, 1980, and 2000 is illustrated in Figure 4. It is clear from these maps that the population of the seventeen counties has become increasingly urban.

Demographic Characteristics

Population pyramids by county and a racial composition map illustrate the age-sex structure and the ethnic composition of the

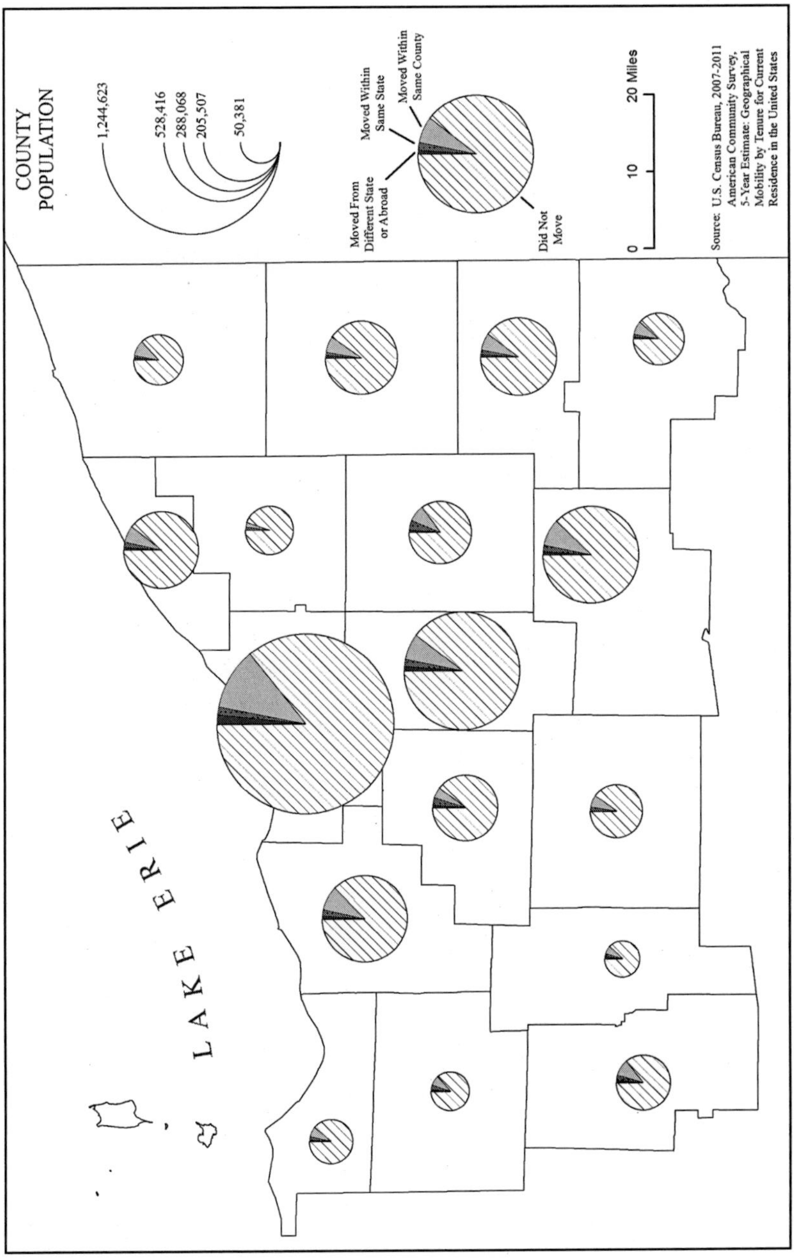

Figure 3. Migration, 2007–2011.

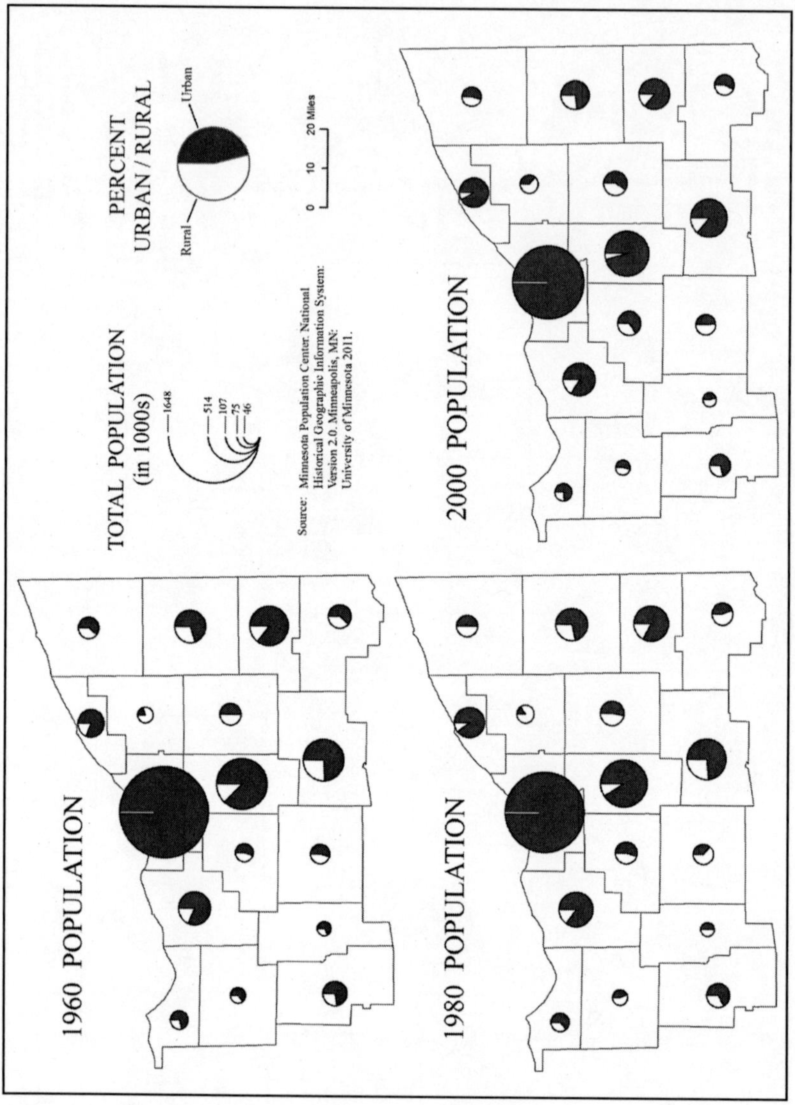

Figure 4. Population change and urban/rural distribution.

population (Figs. 5 and 6). Population pyramids showing the percentage of the total male and female populations by age cohorts indicate that relatively few people are seventy years and older. The male component of the population in the age cohorts more than seventy years is particularly small.

Although the component of the population in the age group from zero to nine is similar in most counties, Cuyahoga County has an extremely narrow base (10 percent) when compared to other counties, due largely to suburbanization. For the same reason, Medina County has a high proportion of its population in the 10 to 19 age group (20 percent). In Portage County, the presence of Kent State University accounts for the high percentage of people in the 20 to 29 age group.

The racial composition of the population in Northeast Ohio is representative of the state distribution and averages. Historically, the black component of the population in Ohio has grown steadily. In 2010, the black or African American population numbered 1,407,681 or 12.2 percent of the total population of the state of Ohio. In Northeast Ohio, there were 609,181 blacks in 2010, or 14.36 percent of the total population of the region. In 1980, the number for blacks was 527,515 blacks or 12.1 percent. In 2010, the number of Hispanics in this area was 101,128 or 2.39 percent. In 1980, the number of Hispanics was 57,664 Hispanics, or 1.3 percent. A high proportion of the black and Hispanic population resides in the inner city (Fig. 6).

In comparison, the white component of the population increases significantly in relation to distance from the city center. Its highest levels are in the outer reaches of Cuyahoga County and the areas around Akron, Canton, and Youngstown (Fig. 6).

Ethnicity, defined as a sense of belonging based on place of origin, language, religion, and common historical memory, has played a salient role in Northeast Ohio, especially in the predominantly urban centers of this region. According to 2012 data from the

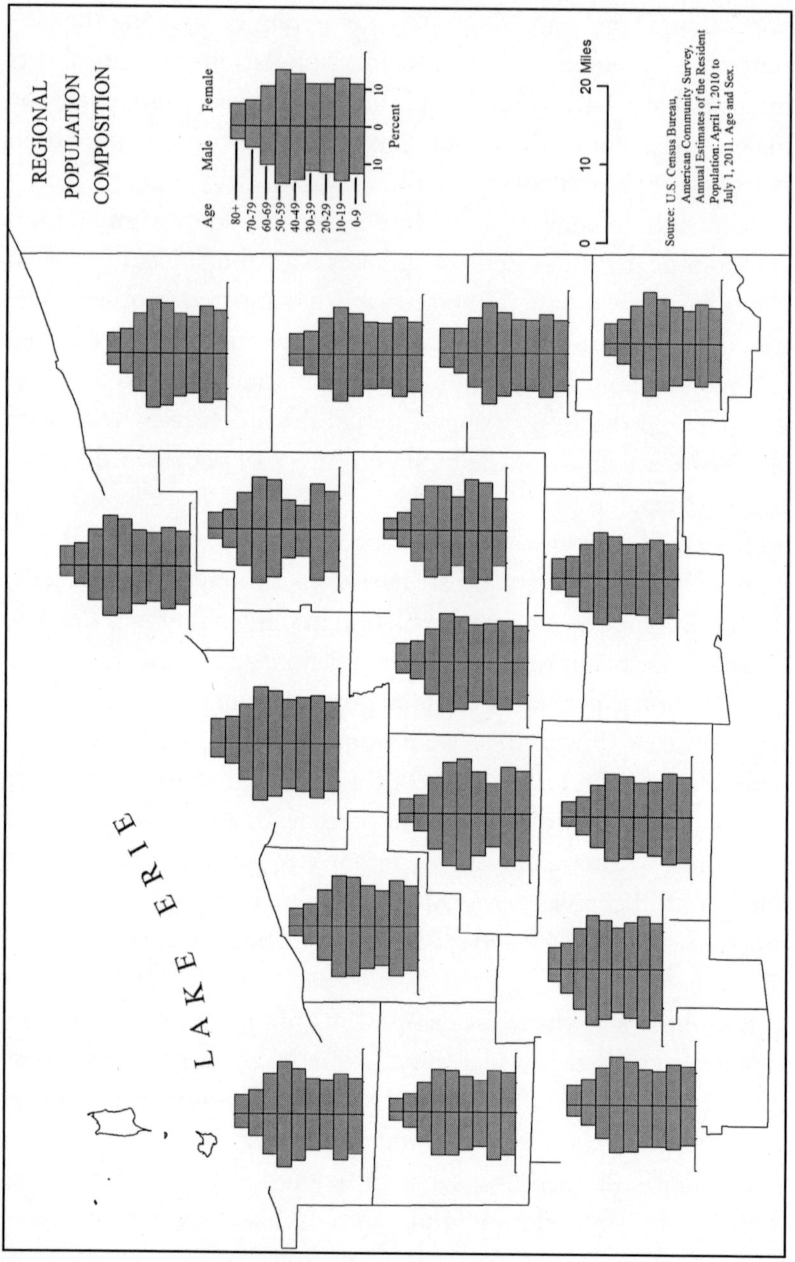

Figure 5. Age and sex characteristics.

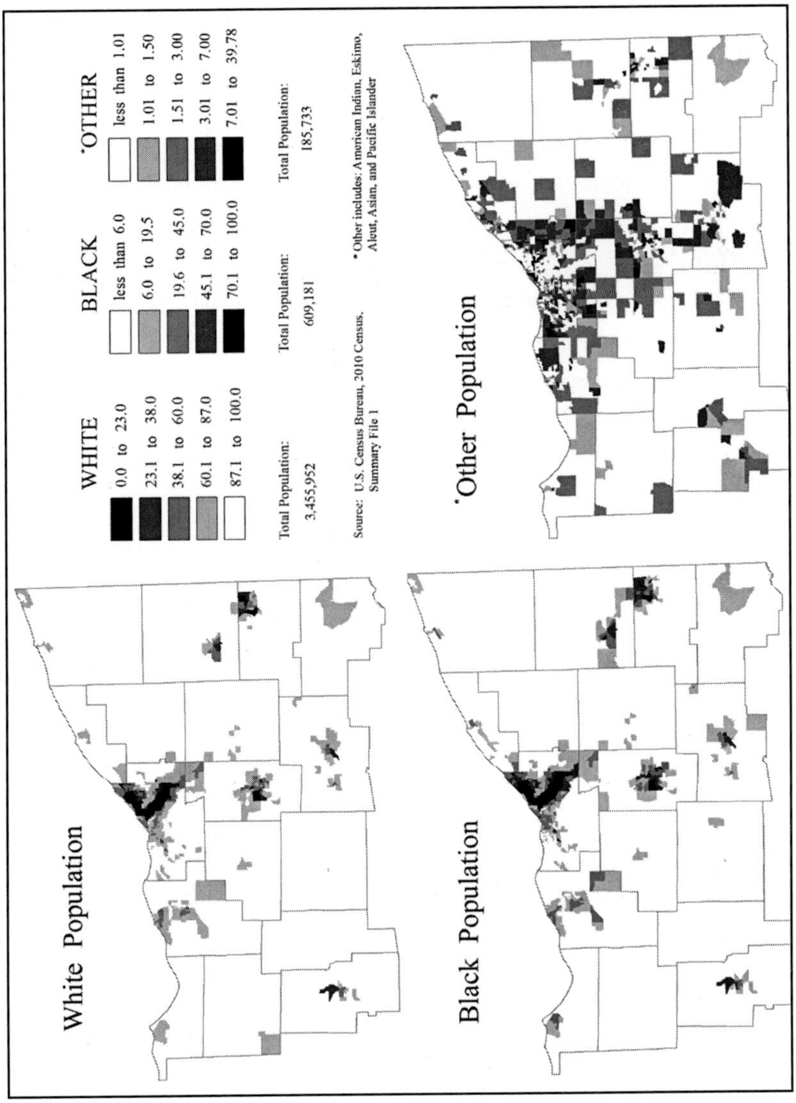

Figure 6. Racial composition in percent.

American Community Survey (ACS), the five largest ancestry groups in Ohio and the United States were the German, Irish, English, American, and Italian (Fig. 7). The category American refers to people who identified their ancestry as American, United States, as a region such as Southerner, or as a US state such as Texan.

Future Change

Certain areas in Northeast Ohio have been growing at significant rates, while others have remained stable and some of them even declined during the period 2000 to 2011 (Fig. 8). The highest growth has been registered by cities, townships, and villages on the outer boundaries of Summit, Medina, Lorain, and Cuyahoga counties. The following communities registered population increases in excess of 100 percent: Lakemore in Summit County, Medina Township in Medina County, Grafton in Lorain County, Monroe Falls in Summit County, Montville Township in Medina County, and Glenwillow in Cuyahoga County. Another area of significant growth is Lorain County which includes Avon, Sheffield Village, North Ridgeville, and Avon Lake. A different cluster of significant growth extends from Portage County to Geauga to Lake County. This cluster comprises the following communities: Tallmadge, Brimfield Township, and Rootstown in Portage County; Auburn Township, Middlefield, Parkman Township, and Hambden Township in Geauga County; and Lakeline and Concord Township in Lake County. Another growth area is the southern tier of Wayne County, which includes Salt Creek Township, Paint Township, and Franklin Township. This area appears as an anomaly, but closer examination reveals that this corridor has a large Amish population. Given that the average size of the Amish family is seven children—at least twice the average size—it is no surprise that this area has such a high growth rate.[15] Finally, there is an area of significant growth in Ashland County which includes the townships of Sullivan, Montgomery, Orange, and Clear Creek. Surrounding these areas of significant growth are narrow

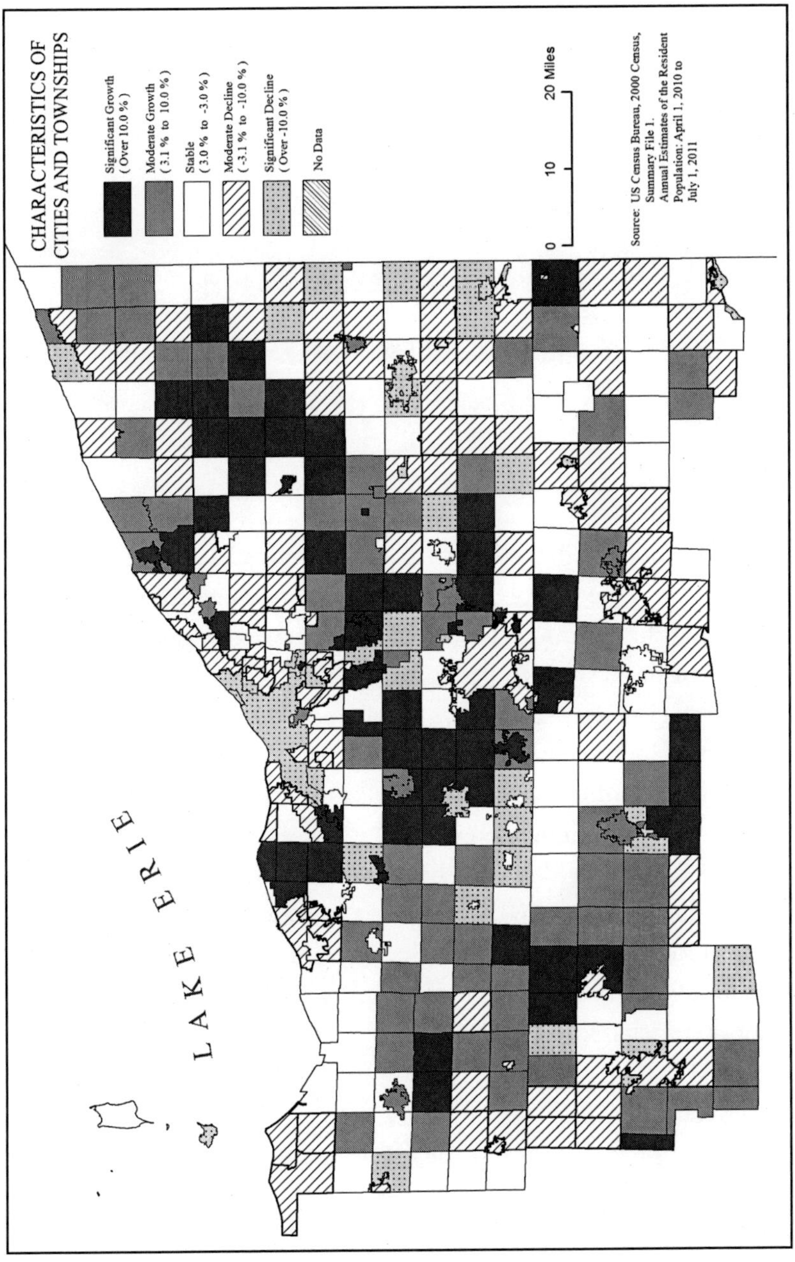

Figure 7. Rate of population change, 2000–2011.

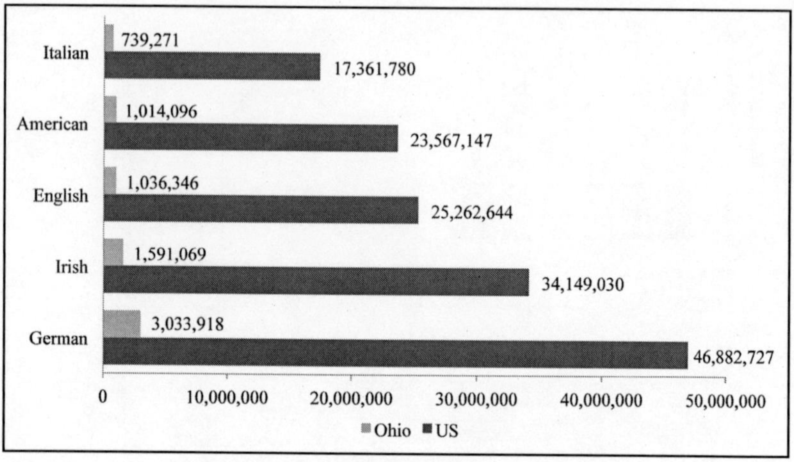

Figure 8. Top Five Ancestry Groups in US and Ohio

zones of moderate growth. These can be viewed as the result of the spillover from the neighboring major metropolitan centers (Fig. 8).

Among the communities which have been experiencing negative growth of more than 50 percent were the following: Hudson and Macedonia in Summit County, Medina in Medina County, Norton in Wayne County, and Hartville Township in Stark County.

The metropolitan corridor from Cleveland to Canton and the outlying metropolitan centers of Mansfield, Youngstown-Warren, and Lorain-Elyria also have been experiencing moderate decline (Fig. 8). Despite the small decline in the region's population during the period from 2000 to 2010, the accelerated urban sprawl that is now underway in several areas has created the broad outlines for an emerging megalopolis.

Acknowledgments

The author wishes to thank Johnathan Kirk for making the maps for this chapter.

References

Hostetler, John A. *Amish Society*. 3rd ed. Baltimore: Johns Hopkins University Press, 1980.

Minnesota Population Center. *National Historical Geographic Information System: Version 2*. Minneapolis, MN: University of Minnesota, 2011. *Percentage Rural Non-Farm Population*, table 1960_cPop; *Urban/Rural Status*, table 1980_STF1; and Population by Urban and Rural, table 2000 _SF1a. https://www.nhgis.org/ (accessed May 7, 2013).

Statistics Canada. "Population and Dwelling Counts for Canada, Provinces and Territories, Census Divisions, and Census Subdivisions (Municipalities), 2011 and 2006 Censuses." *Population and Dwelling Counts, Canada, Provinces and Territories, 2011 and 2006 censuses*. Catalogue number 98-310-XWE2011002 in Statistics Canada [database online]. Ottawa, Ont., 2011. http://www12.statcan.gc.ca/census-recensement/2011/dp-pd/hlt-fst/pd-pl/Table-Tableau.cfm?LANG=Eng&T=304&PR=35&S=51&O=A&RPP=10 (accessed May 7, 2013).

US Census Bureau. "Geographical Mobility in the Past Year by Tenure for Current Residence in the United States." *American FactFinder. 2007–2011 American Community Survey, 5-Year Estimates*. Table B07013. http://factfinder2.census.gov/faces/tableservices/jsf/pages/productview.xhtml?pid=ACS_11_5YR_B07013&prodType=table (accessed May 7, 2013).

US Census Bureau. "Population, Housing Units, Area, and Density: 2010—County / County Equivalent." *American FactFinder. 2010 Census Summary File 1*. Table GCT-PH1. US Census Bureau, 2010. http://factfinder2.census.gov/faces/tableservices/jsf/pages/productview.xhtml?pid=DEC_10_SF1_GCTPH1.ST05&prodType=table (accessed May 7, 2013).

US Census Bureau. "Profile of General Demographic Characteristics: 2000." *American FactFinder. Census 2000 Summary File 1 (SF1) 100% Data*. Table DP-1. US Census Bureau, 2000. http://factfinder2.census.gov/faces/tableservices/jsf/pages/productview.xhtml?pid=DEC_00_SF1_DP1&prodType=table (accessed May 7, 2013).

US Census Bureau. "Profile of General Population and Housing Characteristics: 2010" *American FactFinder. Census 2010 Summary File 1*. Table DP-1. US Census Bureau, 2010. http://factfinder2.census.gov/faces/tableservices/jsf/pages/productview.xhtml?pid=DEC_10_SF1_SF1DP1&prodType=table (accessed May 7, 2013).

US Census Bureau. "Total Ancestry Reported. Universe: Total ancestry categories tallied for people with one or more ancestry categories reported more information 2012 American Community Survey 1-Year Estimates." Table B04003. Washington, DC: US Census Bureau, 2012 American Community Survey. http://factfinder2.census.gov/faces/tableservices/jsf/pages/productview.xhtml?pid=ACS_12_1YR_B04003&prodType=table (Accessed 9/5/2014)

US Census Bureau. "Glossary. The Glossary contains words and terms that you will need to know as you navigate through American FactFinder." http://factfinder2.census.gov/help/en/american_factfinder_help.htm #glossary/glossary.htm

US Census Bureau. Population Division. "Annual Estimates of the Resident Population for Selected Age Groups by Sex: April 1, 2010 to July 1, 2011" *American FactFinder. 2011 Population Estimates*. Table PEPAGESEX. US Census Bureau, 2012. http://factfinder2.census.gov/faces/tableservices/jsf /pages/productview.xhtml?pid=PEP_2011_PEPAGESEX&prodType =table (accessed May 7, 2013).

US Census Bureau. Population Division. "Table 4. Annual Estimates of the Resident Population for Minor Civil Divisions in Ohio, by County: April 1, 2010 to July 1, 2011 (SUB-EST2011-04-39)." *Census 2010. Population Estimates. Annual Estimates of the Resident Population for Minor Civil Divisions, by County: April 1, 2010 to July 1, 2011*. http://www.census.gov /popest/data/cities/totals/2011/tables/SUB-EST2011-04-39.csv (accessed May 7, 2013).

The Road Less Traveled
One Woman's View

Marjorie Carlson Hurst

The western world has seen positive movement in feminism that dates back to the late eighteenth century. In the United States, each decade has seen women who work to overcome the cultural restrictions of over 150 years of gender bias. If you compare the movement of women in business to the innovation of technology, very quickly you could become discouraged and believe the changes have been negligible. Like the analogy of waiting for a glacier to move, the progress is slow and unpredictable and sometimes negligible to the naked eye.

I particularly like the change in language when we discuss women in business. The early women of the '60s were often referred to as "women's libbers." The concept of "bra burners" and women who were out to prove themselves as "good as men" had a pejorative meaning for many of us. We did see a language shift as the attitudes began to slowly improve towards females that stepped away from the traditional role. By the '80s, we were thought of as pioneers or trail blazers which was all well and good and not as negative a stereotype. Today, we are "entrepreneurs." The traits and characteristics of the woman entrepreneur are the same for many. We are women who are risk takers, have a sense of wonder for the possibilities, and generally, can keep a sense of humor about the experiences and the people we encounter along the journey.

For some women the decision to step out of the line and move forward is a cause. For some it is an occurrence that just happens. For most of us, the motivation is the same. It is about economics; plain and simple, economics. You are about to read of my experiences. I fall into the latter category. My career started purely as a happenstance.

Forty Years Riding the Glacier

In the early '70s, the United States was in the throes of implementing Title VII of the Civil Rights Act of 1964. The law was designed to eliminate employment discrimination. The Equal Employment Opportunity Commission (EEOC) was formed and charged with reducing acts of discrimination against minority persons and women. Quickly, the EEOC was engulfed with activities that resulted in litigation against some of the largest and most respected US companies. One of the 1973 settlements was with AT&T. AT&T agreed to distribute $30 million for underpayments of back wages and for pay increases to twenty-five thousand minority and women managers.[16] The phone monopoly committed to "do better" and make hiring decisions that favored the minority applicants.

I began my professional career at The Ohio Bell Telephone Company, a wholly owned subsidiary of AT&T, in January of 1974. At that time, the decision was not surrounded by entrepreneurial spirit or entrepreneurial drive it was based on that other "e" word, economics. Needing to have a career that paid well and provided job security, I entered the job market with optimism and enthusiasm. Not based on desire or skill, I was hired as a lineman.

My employment was the result of government intervention and litigation designed to right decades of wrongs engineered by legacy management, their practices and unwritten policies. I know that now; at the time, I was naive and thought that being hired for a nontraditional career was determined by my aptitude test scores. My story was not an isolated incident. Many women in the '60s and '70s began their careers as the result of an act of government regulation rather than the purity of the concept of equal employment opportunity. Many of the women and minorities were intentional about using EEO to their advantage and many, like in my case, were victims of the circumstances; a happenstance of time and place.

The early '70s represented a challenging time for most women in business, regardless of the corporate level. As a nontraditional laborer in the predominantly male telephony industry, there are many stories that might entertain and amuse the reader. One of the earliest issues a female lineman had to contend with was wardrobe. I was handed a list of required attire in the OBT employment office, which at first glance appeared to be standard items—and today, the items might well be. In the '70s manufacturers did not make clothing for women in the construction field. An example was steel toe boots. Red Wing Shoe Company, leading maker of men's boots did not have a line of steel toe boots to fit the average woman's foot. In order to fulfill the requirement for boots, a special order was placed with the Minnesota factory to ship the smallest men's size and narrowest width to a local store. Upon delivery, the boots were two sizes too big and two widths too wide. They made multiple layers of socks and felt liners a fashion statement not to be denied.

My first months on a line crew were met with resentful men who challenged, ignored, teased, and tormented. I experienced everything from being thrown into a muddy trench of icy water in February to relentless harassment about my pole climbing technique. Little did I know that this was a training ground that could not be provided by any other method. The long physical days primed my thinking and set a foundation for a leadership approach that has sustained a thirty-five year career of nontraditional roles and responsibilities. Those early adventures taught me to work hard, learn more than what was expected of me, look for ways to creatively problem-solve and improve my performance, stay positive, and above all, keep a sense of humor. These lessons came after many trials and tests.

Who could blame the actions of the men that were forced to accept me into their clan? Did I say clan? Yes, it was a clan mentality. There was a perceived kinship that was palatable when an outsider entered their midst. The conversation stopped and an uncomfortable silence could stretch into long periods of time. Glances around the room between the linesmen told a story of resentment, distrust, and rejection. The glacial ice was real and palatable.

Years of the status quo had established a work environment that represented a classic example of "groupthink." Groupthink was a term created by social psychologist Irving Janis as he tried to analyze some historical bad group decisions.[17] According to Janis, groupthink occurred when members had a similar background and insulated themselves from opinions that might challenge their determined group norms. Groupthink occurs when groups are highly cohesive. Groups affected by groupthink ignore alternatives and tend to take irrational actions that dehumanize other groups [or in my case, individuals].[18] Janis documented eight symptoms of groupthink:

1. Illusion of invulnerability—Creates excessive optimism that encourages taking extreme risks.
2. Collective rationalization—Members discount warnings and do not reconsider their assumptions.
3. Belief in inherent morality—Members believe in the rightness of their cause and therefore ignore the ethical or moral consequences of their decisions.
4. Stereotyped views of out-groups—Negative views of "enemy" make effective responses to conflict seem unnecessary.
5. Direct pressure on dissenters—Members are under pressure not to express arguments against any of the group's views.
6. Self-censorship—Doubts and deviations from the perceived group consensus are not expressed.
7. Illusion of unanimity—The majority view and judgments are assumed to be unanimous.
8. Self-appointed 'mindguards'—Members protect the group and the leader from information that is problematic or contradictory to the group's cohesiveness, view, and/or decisions.

The environment at Ohio Bell was not unique for the time period. The traditional roles of men and women were long-standing. Our culture and environment fed and supported the groupthink mentality. For women who selected the conventional thinking of the day, the man works and the woman cares for the household, it took more than just an entrepreneurial spirit. It often took thick skin and a willingness to accept ridicule and rejection. As a female in a non-traditional role, you had to overcome the negative attitudes of your workmates and their life mates. Other females were often less than supportive. They were suspicious of women who worked side-by-side with their spouse.

The Fall Came before the Rise

As my physical abilities grew on the 1974 line crew so did my desire to succeed. It appeared that there would be opportunities to learn about this industry and what better way than from the ground up? Although skeptical, the men that I worked with every day began to lighten up. They came to realize that I would work alongside of them and I did not expect any special treatment. This was a crucial lesson. Much later in my career I could look back and say that during those formative work years, the concept of never asking someone to do something that you yourself would not do was a leadership principle that provided a stepping stone to many subsequent successes.

Looking back, there was one cloudy March day that I can point to and say was pivotal in my career. I had just passed the ninety day probationary period established by the phone company. The line crew still had the jury out on me, but this particular day we were outside of town to set a new telephone pole. The pole had been lying in a ditch and was ice and mud covered on the one side. My three crew mates and I used the auger to drill the four foot hole and set the pole. The next task was to climb the pole and drill a hole to attach a guide cable back to the ground. The men determined that I should climb the pole and drill the hole.

As was my habit before climbing, I removed the small sledge hammer that was normally positioned dead center on my belt in the back. I removed any other tools that I would not need for the task.

Climbing a pole with spurs and carrying the extra weight made climbing more difficult. If you have never climbed a telephone pole as I suspect might be the case for most, you climb to sixteen feet before you belt in. Your goal is to climb, bent at the waist so that you are not parallel to the pole. If you are too straight, you run the risk of the gaffs cutting out of the pole, causing a fall. Climbing requires steady motions and carefully following the training instructors' directions. When you get to working height, you hold yourself with one hand, unsnap one end of the strap-in belt, pass it around the pole to your other hand, and snap it to the other side of your tool belt.

That day was like most and the task was routine. What I had not anticipated was the effect that the ice and mud would have on my gloves. As I reached working height and firmed my one-handed grip to belt in, the hand on the muddy pole slipped and caused me to fall backwards to the frozen ground. The impact of the fall knocked me out. I came to with the sounds of voices saying, "Is she dead?", "Did we kill her?", and "Should we call Charlie (the foreman)?"

That fall earmarked the change in my life and career. I moved from the line crew the following week to a position in a central office. Lest you think that this was an office environment with typewriters, filing cabinets, and the secretarial pool—wrong. I was called an apparatus man or the slang title, "frame jockey." I worked on a crew that ran the physical connections to make phones work at the subscribers' homes. Still considered a nontraditional position, this work was less physical and required a great deal of classroom and on the job training. Aptitude and Bell System training awoke a new desire within me. The world of telephony was fascinating. I learned to read electrical blueprints, to trace circuits, to troubleshoot, and to perform routine maintenance on central office equipment. I moved from being known as the "girl who fell off the pole" to the "best central office troubleshooter." The rise and fall, with the fall coming first…

Moore's law is the concept that technology changes every 18 to 24 months. The telephone industry is proof of Moore's law. As technology changes, there are career changes and options to be considered. Workers can select to fight the changes and end up unemployed; they can retool their skills and move with the industry; or, they can retrain and change career directions. In the late '70s, local phone office operations were being centralized and many of the long-standing roles for workers were threatened. Faced with unemployment, the retool or retrain choice, I selected to retrain.

The advantage of working for a large Fortune 500 company is the vast opportunities that an organization with substantial size and reach can offer. In 1978, trading a tool belt for a briefcase was still considered within the category of nontraditional careers. I moved to the marketing department where a few women could be found in roles other than assistants or secretaries to the male salesmen. If I thought the life of a female lineman was a challenge, I was totally unprepared for two astonishing conditions I encountered in the white collar world.

First was the rather fatherly attitude from the male managers. It was indeed a major shift from the blue collar rejection mode I had left. Male coworkers and senior managers were open to train, to coach, and to help. After many years and several promotions I had an opportunity at a social event to comment on the receptive environment I was experiencing to a sales and marketing vice president. He chuckled and responded, "Well of course, you work hard, do a good job, and we know that you will never make it to our level in the company." I was stunned into silence. There was little doubt that the groupthink mentality was not limited to the labor pool; it was pervasive.

It was well into the '90s, some fifteen years later before women broke through to the senior executive levels. Greater strides have been made in the twenty-first century. In 2014, AT&T was named for the fourth consecutive year by The National Association for Female Executives (NAFE) to its annual list of the top fifty companies for executive women. This recognition focuses a spotlight on companies for their inclusion of women in leadership positions.[19] In 2014, AT&T proclaimed that their workforce is 38 percent female, or in round numbers, ninety thousand women out of a workforce of 233,400 employees.[20]

The second factor that came as a surprise was the way women treated each other. One would have expected solidarity amongst the small ranks but quite the opposite was true. There was an undertone of competitiveness and an effort to one up other females in the office. Often information was not shared or only partial information was provided. Male managers easily pitted female sales representative against female sales representative. Most of the activities were covert until the desired result was achieved and then a form of office bullying might ensue for weeks. Egged on by the male sales representatives, the lack of gender support was a visceral action.

This is a good point to inject one key piece of advice to anyone with career aspirations. Early on, develop a long-term career plan. For women this often has to include breaks for children and other family responsibilities. Without an end goal or achievement in mind, you can become unfocused and you can get derailed easily. Determine the steps that will be necessary to take you to your end goal. Identify the risks that could knock you off the path. Based on those risks, look at the likelihood of them happening and the seriousness of their consequences. Every challenge has risks and if you go blindly without careful and thorough analysis, your probability of success is lowered. After you have taken the time to focus on risks, you can develop a plan for mitigating these career challenges.

At one point in my career, I was told by a manager that if a promotion was between a male colleague and me, and all things were equal, he would select the male. Protesting such statements would not solve the problem; it would not put me in favor or good graces of the leadership team. What his admission did was offer a solution. The solution was that I had to find a differentiator and keep that differentiator. Education was one tool that I selected to add to my resume. I attended seminars, company training, and sought out respected mentors both inside and outside the organization. I was accepted into an Executive MBA Program and then went on to finish doctoral studies. I studied leadership and industry trends. All in all, it helped keep me ahead of the curve and often better informed than my competition. Education was one of the steps that I used as a mitigating factor in the gender roadblock.

Second Career Transitions

Throughout the twenty-five years of working for a monopoly, experiencing divestiture, learning to work in a competitive environment, processing the effects of Moore's law, and adapting to constant change all prepared me in many ways to transition from corporate America to the other side of the classroom lectern. When the call came from my alma mater that they were looking for a key academic leader to help with an institutional-wide reorganization and take some specific programs to the next level, I felt amazingly well prepared.

Moving from the business world to the world of academia in 2000 was not without interesting challenges. The academy presented a strange conundrum that took me by surprise. There were still some chasms that were difficult to bridge. It was a curiosity to see very educated people who still harbored stereotypes. The biases were often less about gender or race, but were instead focused on discipline, credentials, degrees, and degree-awarding universities. The fight for acceptance continues…

Conclusion

Throughout a long and delightfully colorful career, I have often thought of myself as a trailblazer and a pioneer; both are frequently used as synonyms for an entrepreneur. There is a difference from my perspective. The trailblazers or pioneers have another dimension that is different from entrepreneurship. Being an entrepreneur is about achieving one's vision. A trailblazer marks the way and cuts the path for others to follow. Pioneers take risks into the unknown to advance their position. From one trailblazing pioneer's perspective "nothing hard is easy" and "every plan has a price." As you step forward into the unknown, the power of grasping opportunity, regardless of how foreign it may feel at the time, will propel you into the future and take you places even your plan could not foresee. The progress is slow in retrospect, but the progress each woman makes will help the world to change and make equality more of a reality for those who follow.

References

AT&T News (2014). https://www.att.com/gen/corporate-citizenship?pid=17725

Janis, Irving L. (1982). Groupthink: Psychological Studies of Policy Decisions and Fiascoes. Second Edition. New York: Houghton Mifflin.

Milestones in History (1974). http://www.eeoc.gov/eeoc/history/35th/milestones/1974.html

NAFE Homepage (2014). http://www.nafe.com/?service=vpage/1474.

Ways Northeast Ohio Can Support Innovation

Northeast Ohio was the center of innovation in the late 1800s and early 1900s with the rubber and tire industry in Akron and with steel, shipping, and finance in Cleveland. A lot of wealth was created here. But, the decline of the past century has had a dramatic effect on the local economy and on the way people invest their wealth. I think the wealthy may have become more concerned with preservation rather than growth. For example, we now look to outside venture capital to support entrepreneurial endeavors. Why can't we convince the descendants of the last century's entrepreneurs to fund the growth here? The colleges and universities are doing a great job innovating, but their funding is now waning. The federal government cannot afford as much funding for research, so colleges and universities need to look elsewhere. I don't know how to solve these dilemmas, but they need to be dealt with.

—John M. Finley II, Founder, MemPro Ceramics Corporation (Akron)

Facilitate independent evaluation of technology, make opportunities from within universities known, support internal team-building, and provide access to strategic partners and specialists. Don't assume others can do it better.

—Lauren Wolf, CEO, AeroClay, Inc. (Cleveland)

Our culture here for entrepreneurs is a strange one. We have pockets of innovators and entrepreneurs who will fully support young talent, but on the other side we still have a poor environment for young entrepreneurs. I was once told, while pursuing a source of grant funding, that the organization wouldn't invest in someone my age no matter what the idea was.

—Christopher Clark, CEO, Sunflower Solutions (Shaker Heights)

Ways Northeast Ohio Can Support Innovation (cont'd.)

Develop activities and institutions that are appealing to creative young people just starting their careers. This means more activity in the fields of entertainment, video, film, design, animation, photography, art, and music.

—Mitchell Kahan, Director Emeritus, Akron Art Museum

For the past six years I have volunteered as a counselor for SCORE, Counselors to America's Small Business. It is one of a number of Northeast Ohio organizations in support of entrepreneurial activities. In my opinion, we already have in place organizations such as JumpStart, ARCHAngels, SCORE, SBA, and the universities and colleges where people can go for start-up help. So, I don't think there is a money problem. Rather, it is an idea problem.

—Russ Vernon, Retired Chairman, West Point Market (Akron)

I love that there is so much funding coming to this region between the government and nonprofits, yet it is all being wasted. A group like JumpStart has a $13 million budget, but they use $10 million on overhead and only invest $3 million. This is backwards! Most of the regional organizations operate on less than $2 million for overhead. That $10 million needs to be invested in people with the right experience and qualifications, who are creating companies, and who can make returns on those investments.

—Mike Burkons, Founder, Charitee Golf LLC (Shaker Heights)

Northeast Ohio can attract foreign talent, advertise a broad local lifestyle and affordability to top inventors who are reluctant to move to other centers, and they can give incentives to people who move in.

—Damir Janigro, Cleveland Clinic Foundation and Cofounder, Flocel, Inc. (Cleveland)

Ways Northeast Ohio Can Support Innovation (cont'd.)

We should go back to elementary, middle, and high school levels. Their curriculum needs to be revamped so it is innovation-oriented. There needs to be an emphasis on thinking outside of the box. Continue the development of the innovation-friendly curriculum in higher education, especially in the engineering and business programs in colleges.

—*Majid Rashidi, Professor, Cleveland State University*

I think we need to find a better balance between supporting existing industries and encouraging innovation and entrepreneurship to develop future industries. There doesn't seem to be any voice within our society encouraging people to start a new business themselves. This lack of encouragement for entrepreneurialism in our society comes from the fact that this is a region where older, more established industries have flourished.

—*Neil Sater, Cofounder, GreenField Solar (Oberlin)*

There are so many positive aspects in doing business in Northeast Ohio and this is why, although I am often courted by companies to establish operations in other parts of the world, I am truly committed to building my global business here. So many people in our community have helped me along the way and have done so, not from the positions in which they work, but from their heart and their true desire to support my vision. I would like to see our educational system continue to develop programs that encourage entrepreneurship and also build the key technical skill sets that are required to support advanced manufacturing and technology companies in the future.

—*Hiroyuki Fujita, President & CEO, Quality Electrodynamics (Mayfield Village)*

Employment Characteristics

Thomas A. Maraffa and Thomas A. Finnerty

The labor force and employment structure of the Northeast Ohio region represents a microcosm of the broader region in which it is located, a region formally known as the Manufacturing Belt but popularly given the moniker Rust Belt. In other words, Northeast Ohio has experienced stagnant employment growth, the erosion of its manufacturing base, and the transition to a labor force in which a variety of service occupations dominate the occupations of its population.

These changes are the result of a combination of external and internal forces. Externally, these include the rise of globalization and the resultant shift of US manufacturing to foreign locations, especially those with growing local markets and lower cost structures. Within the US, the competitiveness of the region has suffered as the United States has transitioned to a postindustrial economy and the locational factors that have historically favored the region have given way to such location factors as access to research universities, climate and other natural and cultural amenities, and the relatively low influence of labor unions and other aspects of labor climate, all of which favor the part of the US known as the Sun Belt. The construction of the system of limit access highways has both made the region more accessible to the country as a whole and facilitated longer distance commuting to work within the region.

During the first decade of the twenty-first century, both Northeast Ohio and the state suffered through declining employment. In 1997 the region employed 1.84 million but by 2011 total employment in the region declined to 1.76 million, a loss of eighty thousand jobs or 4.3 percent. During the same period employment in Ohio fell from 4.7 million to 4.3 million, a decline of 8.5 percent. Northeast Ohio accounted for 39 percent of the state's employment in 1997 and 41 percent in 2011. Both of these percentages are an increase over the 35 percent share of the state's employment in the region in 1980.

During the past thirty years, the occupational structure of the region has evolved as one would expect given the economic restructuring during this period. In the early 1980s, 35 percent of the region's labor force was employed in manufacturing with the remaining 65 percent evenly distributed between three broad categories: services, retailing, and a broad grouping that includes wholesaling, transportation, finance, insurance, real estate, and contract construction. Currently, only 14 percent of the region's labor force is employed in manufacturing, representing 242,000 workers.

The impact of the decline in manufacturing is particularly striking in those counties where manufacturing was even more dominant than it was in the region as a whole. In the early 1980s, manufacturing represented approximately 50 percent of the employment in three counties in the region: Trumbull, Huron, and Ashland. Today in these relatively small counties, the percentage of employment in manufacturing in each county is 20 percent, 31 percent, and 22 percent respectively. The 31 percent share represents the highest percentage in the region.

Health care and social services are now the largest category, employing 23 percent of the region's labor force and over 408,000 people. The growth of the health care sector mirrors state and national trends but can be further explained by the aging of the region's population, increasing the demand for health care services, and the fact that the region's major health care providers such as the Cleveland Clinic draw patients from beyond the region. Health care accounts for between 25 percent and 30 percent of the labor force in nine of the regions counties: Erie, Lorain, Mahoning, Medina, Richland, Stark, Summit, and Trumbull. These are counties that thirty years ago had the greatest dependence on manufacturing employment.

Retailing, wholesaling, and other services account for 31 percent of the labor force. The distribution of employment in these sectors generally is associated with that of the region's population. Overall retailing represents 12 percent of the region's labor force, but in no county is it more than 17 percent. The counties with the highest proportion of retail employment—Medina, Portage, and Columbiana—are adjacent to central city counties.

Government employment accounts for 6 percent of the regions jobs and over 113,000 workers. Government employment is particularly concentrated in Cuyahoga County which accounts for over half of the public sector employment in the region. Sixteen thousand of the twenty-five thousand federal jobs are located in Cuyahoga County.

One can interpret these shifts in occupational restructure as the region evolving toward a more diversified economy. However, it also represents the loss of higher paid manufacturing jobs. Many health care occupations and public sector employment provide compensation comparable to that found in industrial occupations. However, as in the state and the nation, many service occupations pay well below the above categories and offer little in the way of benefits.

The future occupational structure of Northeast Ohio will be influenced by several evolving trends. First, is that health care and public sector employment are supported by transfer payments from governments and between private and public insurance agencies and health care providers. An open question is the extent that these transfer payments can be supported in the future and the resulting impact on employment. Second, is that the region has developed a presence in what is called advanced manufacturing in areas such as polymers, ceramics, and technology. It remains to be seen whether the number of jobs created will have a measurable impact on the region's economy. Third, the region is within the emerging natural gas development zone. While optimistic projections of the impact of the development of natural gas on the region's economy have been put forth, it remains to be seen if these will actually materialize. Finally, there have been notable efforts to position Northeast Ohio as part of an integrated urban region extending from Cleveland to Pittsburgh known as the Tech Belt. While the concept has potential for long-term employment, in reality it has not evolved beyond the conceptual stage.

The occupational structure of Northeast Ohio, at the end of the first decade of the twenty-first century, is defined by the decline of manufacturing and the emergence of the health care sector. While the manufacturing economy was dependent on external markets and the changing geography of production costs, the health care economy is defined by external public policies and transfer payments. In each case, the challenge was and remains to be competitive and viable in the face of forces beyond the regions control.

Manufacturing in Northeast Ohio

Bruce W. Smith and Neil Reid

Introduction

Similar to many other industrial areas in the American manufacturing belt, manufacturing historically was one of the engines driving the economic growth of Northeast Ohio (Figure 1). Manufacturing remains an important component of the economic base of the area. According to Bureau of Labor Statistics employment data, manufacturing jobs constituted 15.8 percent of total employment in 2010 in the seventeen counties of Northeast Ohio (Table 1). This percentage for Northeast Ohio was larger than the corresponding percentages for Ohio and the US, which were 14.9 percent and 10.8 percent respectively. Thus, Northeast Ohio was more specialized in manufacturing than either Ohio or the nation.

Manufacturing employment was unequally distributed across the region in 2010. Almost 40 percent of the manufacturing jobs were located in Cuyahoga, Summit, and Stark Counties. In 2001, those three counties accounted for 49.1 percent of the region's manufacturing jobs. Despite the diminished percentage contributed by the three large counties, most other counties contributed substantially smaller percentages to the regional manufacturing labor force, such as Ashland, Erie, Columbiana, and Huron, which together contributed less than 8 percent of the regional total in 2010 and 8.5 percent in 2001 (Table 1).

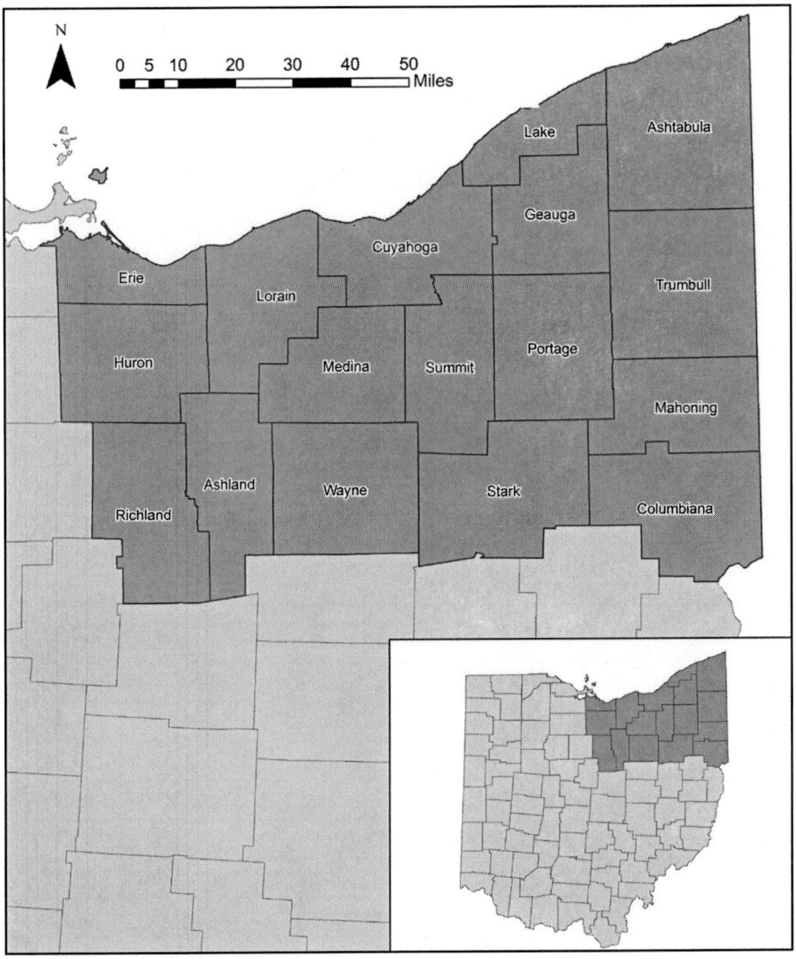

Figure 1. Northeast Ohio

Wide variations in the role of manufacturing in counties' total employment in 2010 can be observed. The lowest percentage of manufacturing in the labor force occurred in Mahoning and Cuyahoga Counties, with values of 9.9 percent and 11.4 percent respectively. In contrast, the industrial structure of Huron and Wayne Counties were more oriented to manufacturing with 31.6 percent and 30.4 percent of their labor forces employed in manufacturing. It is notable that only Mahoning was less specialized in manufacturing than the US; the other sixteen counties had values higher than the national average. Indeed, only three counties in the region (Cuyahoga, Mahoning, and Summit) were less specialized in manufacturing than the state of Ohio. In essence, even though there are wide variations in the distribution of manufacturing within Northeast Ohio, most counties within the region are more specialized in manufacturing than Ohio or the nation (Table 1).

Table 1. Manufacturing Employment Change, 2001–2010

County	Manufacturing Employment		Percent Change in Manufacturing Employment	Manufacturing Share of Total Employment	
	2001	2010	2001–2010	2001	2010
Ashland	5,677	3,084	-45.7%	35.0%	21.5%
Ashtabula	9,257	6,279	-32.2%	32.9%	25.6%
Columbiana	8,327	5,218	-36.1%	29.2%	22.2%
Cuyahoga	107,756	67,107	-37.7%	15.5%	11.4%
Erie	9,044	5,173	-42.8%	26.7%	17.2%
Geauga	9,953	6,944	-30.2%	34.1%	25.2%
Huron	9,939	5,598	-43.6%	42.3%	31.6%
Lake	25,555	18,648	-27.0%	29.3%	23.3%
Lorain	26,061	15,520	-40.4%	29.6%	20.4%
Mahoning	11,836	8,083	-31.7%	12.6%	9.9%
Medina	10,715	8,291	-22.6%	23.1%	16.9%
Portage	13,534	9,374	-30.7%	33.3%	25.2%
Richland	15,486	8,706	-43.8%	30.1%	20.4%
Stark	40,004	23.421	-41.5%	26.0%	18.1%
Summit	43,326	27,973	-35.4%	18.8%	12.6%
Trumbull	26,867	12,656	-52.9%	34.1%	21.1%
Wayne	15,233	10,601	-30.4%	37.0%	30.4%
NE Ohio	388,570	242,676	-37.5%	22.0%	15.8%
Ohio	955,771	620,308	-35.1%	20.4%	14.9%
US	16,386,001	11,487,496	-29.9%	15.0%	10.8%

Source: US Department of Labor, Bureau of Labor Statistics, *Quarterly Census of Employment and Wages, 2010*. (http://www.bls.gov/cew/cewlq.htm).

Like many industrial areas in the northeastern US, the number of manufacturing jobs in the region has been declining in recent years (Table 1). Between 2001 and 2010, Northeast Ohio manufacturing firms lost 145,894 jobs resulting in an employment decline of 37.5 percent from 388,750 to 242,676, compared to a 35.1 percent drop in Ohio and a 29.9 percent decrease in the nation. These losses can be attributed to the shift to a postindustrial society, increased competition from foreign manufacturing, and the redistribution of manufacturing out of the American Manufacturing Belt to other regions in the US. The decline in manufacturing, while not uniform throughout the region, exceeded the national average in all counties, except in the case of Lake and Medina counties. In Trumbull County over 50 percent of the manufacturing jobs were lost. Not surprisingly, the importance of the manufacturing sector as an employer declined significantly during the period in question. Region-wide this share decreased from 22 percent to 15.8 percent between 2001 and 2010. The largest decrease was experienced by Ashland County where the manufacturing sector accounted for 35 percent of the county's employment in 2001 compared to 21.5 percent in 2010; a decrease of 13.5 percentage points. In general, the loss of manufacturing employment was one of the dominant trends in the manufacturing map of Northeast Ohio during the first decade of the twenty-first century.

Leading Industrial Sectors

To protect the confidentiality of company-level information, the Census Bureau suppresses employment information. This usually occurs in the case of small geographic units, such as counties, an industry with few employers, or an industry that is dominated by a single large employer. However, *County Business Patterns* does report information on the number of establishments. Therefore, *County Business Patterns* establishments' data were used to measure the sectoral distribution of manufacturing (Table 2).

Table 2. Distribution of Manufacturing Establishments by Sector

Sector	Northeastern Ohio		Ohio		US	
	2001	2010	2001	2010	2001	2010
Food	4.5%	4.8%	5.4%	5.8%	7.6%	8.3%
Beverage and tobacco	0.4%	0.7%	0.5%	0.7%	0.9%	1.5%
Textile mills	0.5%	0.5%	0.5%	0.4%	1.3%	0.8%
Textile product mills	1.2%	1.2%	1.3%	1.4%	2.0%	2.1%
Apparel	1.2%	0.4%	1.3%	0.5%	4.6%	2.4%
Leather and allied products	0.2%	0.2%	0.2%	0.2%	0.5%	0.4%
Wood products	2.4%	2.3%	3.9%	3.9%	4.9%	4.8%
Paper	1.8%	1.8%	2.2%	2.1%	1.6%	1.5%
Printing and related support activities	4.5%	7.5%	9.1%	8.5%	10.7%	9.7%
Petroleum and coal products	0.8%	1.0%	1.0%	1.0%	0.6%	0.7%
Chemicals	4.1%	4.7%	4.0%	4.6%	3.8%	4.3%
Plastics and rubber products	7.0%	6.7%	6.6%	6.4%	4.5%	4.3%
Nonmetallic mineral products	4.0%	4.2%	4.8%	4.8%	4.7%	5.3%
Primary metals	3.9%	3.1%	3.3%	2.8%	1.9%	1.6%
Fabricated metals	27.2%	28.1%	23.8%	24.6%	17.2%	18.6%
Machinery	13.9%	12.7%	12.3%	11.5%	8.2%	8.1%
Computer and electronic products	2.8%	3.0%	2.9%	3.0%	4.8%	4.4%
Electrical equipment	2.7%	2.6%	2.3%	2.2%	2.0%	2.0%
Transportation equipment	3.5%	3.9%	4.0%	4.5%	3.6%	3.9%
Furniture and related products	3.5%	3.4%	4.2%	4.3%	5.8%	5.8%
Miscellaneous manufacturing	6.3%	7.2%	6.3%	6.9%	8.7%	9.4%
Total	100%	100%	100%	100%	100%	100%

Source: US Department of Commerce, County Business Patterns, 2010. http: www .census.gov/econ/cbp/

The largest industrial sector in Northeast Ohio was fabricated metals manufacturing, which composed 28.1 percent of the region's total manufacturing establishments in 2010. This was followed by machinery manufacturing (12.7 percent of the total). In the case of both of these industries, Northeast Ohio was more specialized than the state of Ohio, in which the sectors respectively composed 24.6 percent and 11.5 percent of the total establishments. Similarly the region is more specialized than the nation in those sectors, where the respective percentages were 18.6 percent and 8.1 percent. Even though it is not a large component of the regional industrial structure, Northeast Ohio is more specialized than the nation in plastics and rubber products, 6.7 percent versus 4.3 percent.

Fabricated metals and machinery manufacturing were unevenly distributed throughout the region in 2010. As one might expect, their distribution is strongly related to the population size of counties. In the case of fabricated metals, Cuyahoga County contained 32.3 percent of the regional total, followed by Lake County (14.1 percent of the total) and Summit County (11.3 percent of the total). Together these three counties contained 57.8 percent of the fabricated metals establishments in the region. The geographic distribution of machinery manufacturing was somewhat similar. The three leading counties were Cuyahoga (29.4 percent of the total), Summit (14.9 percent), and Lake (10 percent), with three counties accounting for 54.3 percent of the region's total establishments. One other notable concentration, albeit smaller in size, is in Summit County which was the leading area of plastics and rubber products manufacturing with almost 20 percent of the regional total.

Despite the substantial loss of manufacturing jobs in Northeast Ohio, the distribution of manufacturing establishments by sector remained relatively stable between 2001 and 2010. In most sectors, the change was less than 1 percent. On the growth side, printing and related support activities increased from 4.5 percent in 2001 to 7.5 percent in 2010. Conversely, machinery manufacturing diminished from 13.9 percent in 2010 to 12.7 percent in 2010. All other changes during the decade were less than 1 percent.

Size Distribution

The size of manufacturing establishments within a region has various impacts. One is their differential role in the generation of employment. While not all experts would agree, many researchers believe that small firms create more jobs than do large firms. In fact, Neumark, Wall, and Zhang not only reported that small firms and small establishments create more jobs, but also there is an inverse relationship in manufacturing between size of operation and job generation.[21] Thus one would expect regions with large numbers of small firms to have higher rates of entrepreneurial activity and job creation.

We defined small as establishments with less than twenty employees. In 2010, Northeast Ohio had a slightly higher percentage of manufacturing establishments than did Ohio (67.1 percent and 66.4 percent respectively) (Table 3). However, the region had a somewhat lower percentage of small establishments than did the nation, which was 71.3 percent.

The occurrence of small manufacturing operations will differ among regions for various reasons, such as market differences, labor availability, and type of industry. Nonetheless, the percentage of manufacturing firms that have less than twenty employees was comparable among the counties of Northeast Ohio, with only 13 percent separating the highest and lowest counties. Mahoning County had the highest percentage at 72.6 percent, whereas the lowest was Trumbull County with a 59.6 percent. To the extent that small manufacturing establishments are an asset for job creation in a region, most counties in Northeast Ohio benefit from a presence of small manufacturing firms and their entrepreneurial activities.

The Innovation Environment

Innovation is one of the cornerstones of a successful manufacturing sector in the twenty-first century. Innovativeness varies from person to person, business to business, and region to region. Examining the innovativeness of individual businesses is outside the scope

Table 3. Geographic Distribution of Small Firms

Area	Percentage of Establishments With Less Than 20 Employees
Ashland County	60.0
Ashtabula County	60.7
Columbiana County	71.7
Cuyahoga County	68.5
Erie County	65.7
Geauga County	66.5
Huron County	61.5
Lake County	71.0
Lorain County	69.6
Mahoning County	72.6
Medina County	65.0
Portage County	59.7
Richland County	62.4
Stark County	65.3
Summit County	66.7
Trumbull County	59.6
Wayne County	64.8
Northeastern Ohio	67.1
Ohio	66.4
US	71.3

Source: US Department of Commerce, County Business Patterns, 2010. http: www.census.gov/econ/cbp/

of this chapter. However, using the Innovation Index from the *Innovations in American Regions* project we are able to make a few observations about the innovation environment within which Northeast Ohio manufacturers are operating.[22]

The Innovation Index compares a county or multicounty region with the United States and produces an index score that provides a relative measure of the innovation environment of that county or region. The benchmark value for the nation is 100 so a score under

100 means the area is lagging the nation. The Innovation Index comprises four components—Human Capital (30 percent), Economic Dynamics (30 percent), Productivity and Employment (30 percent), and Economic Well Being (10 percent). Each component is based upon a number of subcomponents (Table 4). For example, the variables that are used to calculate a county's Productivity and Employment score are change in high tech employment, job growth, GDP per worker, and average patents per worker.

The Innovation Index is not a harbinger of good news for Northeast Ohio. The Innovation Index for the region as a whole is 82.5 (Table 5). This suggests that, compared to the nation as a whole, the region does not have an environment that is conducive to innovative endeavors. Of the four components that comprise the overall Innovation Index, the region scores highest on economic well-being (93.4) and lowest on economic dynamics (78.8).

Table 4. Components of the Innovation Index

Human Capital (30%)	Economic Dynamics (30%)	Productivity & Employment (30%)	Economic Well Being (10%)
Educational Attainment	Average Venture Capital	Change in High Tech Employment	Average Poverty Rate
Population Growth Rate	Broadband Density & Penetration	Job Growth	Average Unemployment Rates
High Tech Employment Share	Establishment Churn	GDP Per Worker	Average Net Migration
Technology-based Occupations	Establishment Sizes	Average Patents per 1,000 Workers	Average Growth in Per Capita Personal Income
			Compensation

Source: Innovation in American Regions http://www.statsamerica.org/innovation/index.html

Despite the generally gloomy picture for the region as a whole, there are some islands of hope within the region. Two counties, Cuyahoga (100.6) and Summit (100.2), have Innovation Index scores that are above 100. Both of those counties score particularly well on the Productivity and Employment component with Cuyahoga County scoring 127.9 and Summit County scoring 132.1. Only one other county, Lorain, has an Innovation Index score greater than 90. Eight of the region's seventeen counties have Innovation Index scores below 80, with the lowest score belonging to Columbiana County (70.4).

Table 5. The Innovation Index

County	Innovation Index	Index Component Scores			
		Human Capital (30%)	Economic Dynamics (30%)	Productivity and Employment (30%)	Economic Well-Being (10%)
Ashland	78.7	73.6	84.2	73.2	93.9
Ashtabula	70.8	61.4	74.4	69.7	91.2
Columbiana	70.4	57.7	77.6	69.1	96.7
Cuyahoga	100.6	91.0	85.3	127.9	93.5
Erie	75.0	65.3	78.3	75.9	91.5
Geauga	85.5	88.3	77.8	86.3	97.4
Huron	77.8	73.8	82.3	73.2	90.2
Lake	87.0	89.9	77.8	90.6	95.4
Lorain	96.9	85.4	80.9	125.4	94.3
Mahoning	76.6	73.1	69.2	81.1	95.4
Medina	80.8	82.2	79.0	75.4	97.8
Portage	70.9	77.6	73.4	82.4	96.7
Richland	78.7	77.1	76.5	78.8	89.5
Stark	83.9	71.4	81.1	95.3	95.7
Summit	100.2	89.7	79.9	132.1	97.2
Trumbull	74.2	67.5	76.7	74.5	85.4
Wayne	82.7	68.7	75.9	100.0	93.4
NE Ohio	82.5	82.9	78.8	82.0	94.2

Source: Innovation in American Regions http://www.statsamerica.org/innovation/index.html

These generally low Innovation Index scores suggest that Northeast Ohio manufacturers will struggle when it comes to competing in innovative activities vis-à-vis the rest of the nation. The region is further hampered in its innovation efforts due to the fact that it is part of Ohio. The Innovation Index also calculates an index called State Context, an index based upon the number of science and engineering graduates per one thousand residents and state R&D expenditures as a percentage of state GDP. This provides a measure of the resources available in a state to entrepreneurs and businesses for entrepreneurial activities. The State Index score for Ohio is 85.8, suggesting that Ohio, compared with the rest of the nation, is not particularly supportive of innovative activities.

Conclusion

Manufacturing employment is a large component of the employment base of Northeast Ohio. Even with the declines between 2001 and 2010, manufacturing remains more concentrated in the region than in Ohio or the US. Not surprisingly, Cuyahoga, Summit, and Stark Counties are the largest centers of manufacturing employment, with fabricated metals manufacturing and machinery manufacturing being the largest manufacturing sectors in the region. The region has a substantial percentage of manufacturing establishments with less than twenty employees, which is positive since many believe operations of that size create more jobs than do large firms. On the negative side of the ledger, the region's Innovation Index lags the nation. However, there are some bright spots, such as Cuyahoga County and Summit County scoring high in the Productivity and Employment component of the index.

References

US Department of Commerce, *County Business Patterns, 2010*. (www.census.gov/econ/cbp/).

US Department of Labor, Bureau of Labor Statistics, *Quarterly Census of Employment and Wages, 2010*. (www.bls.gov/cew/cewlq.htm).

Northeast Ohio

A Region Unites to Encourage and Support Entrepreneurs

Richard J. Batyko

The economy of Northeast Ohio—which includes cities such as Cleveland, Akron, Canton, and Youngstown—is gaining positive momentum. It added more than ten thousand net jobs in 2013. More than $19 billion in new physical development has been initiated since 2010, encompassing the education and health care sectors and expanding the region's corporate, commercial, and entertainment infrastructure. The number of downtown residents has increased 88 percent since 2000, with occupancy rates currently above 94 percent. Many factors are contributing to the region's upswing, but its heritage of entrepreneurship and its forward-thinking approach to fostering start-up companies is certainly a factor.

For example, Cleveland Whiskey CEO and founder Tom Lix moved from Boston to Northeast Ohio several years ago to care for an aging family member. After arriving, this serial entrepreneur began looking for funding and support for a novel idea: accelerating the distillation of whiskey. What he found in the region was a wealth of resources and an inventive spirit. "Here, people are willing to take risks on ideas," he says. "This assistance enabled me to build a laboratory and helped me build prototypes. That wouldn't have happened in Boston."

Besides obtaining funding from the Cuyahoga County North Coast Opportunities Fund (developed by the Cuyahoga County [Ohio] Department of Development) and the Innovation Fund (a regional fund founded by the Lorain County Community College Foundation that's focused on supporting technology-based entrepreneurial endeavors), Cleveland Whiskey found a home at The Incubator at MAGNET, a nonprofit dedicated to growing and advancing manufacturing in Northeast Ohio. The latter's unique support services have made a big difference. "They have mechanical engineers, electrical engineers, robotics experts, people who think outside the box," he enthuses. "They've helped me design my systems."

It Takes A Region

Every region in the United States wants to have its own entrepreneurial successes: young companies that grow to create significant jobs and wealth for their communities. Successes like that require more than good ideas; a region's entrepreneurial ecosystem needs to provide entrepreneurs with the capital, assistance, and networks they need to accelerate their success. And those resources need to work together effectively and efficiently.

According to the Kauffman Foundation, in the last thirty years, all net new job growth in the United States has stemmed from young, high growth companies. Because of this, regions across the country need to find ways to not only build infrastructure that attracts existing companies, but also grows new ones. By doing so, regions can create new jobs. It's a relatively new approach to economic development, but one that is increasingly important.

In 2004, business, civic, and philanthropic leaders in Northeast Ohio formed a nonprofit organization to help the region's entrepreneurs grow their businesses. Called JumpStart, the organization has invested expertise and dollars directly into 76 companies and nurtured another 393 by providing business development advice and connections. As the pipeline of young companies has grown, so has the number of entrepreneurial resources in the region—from accelerators and incubators to angel groups and higher education classes.

This graphic demonstrates how this ecosystem-building approach to entrepreneurship has had an impact on Northeast Ohio:

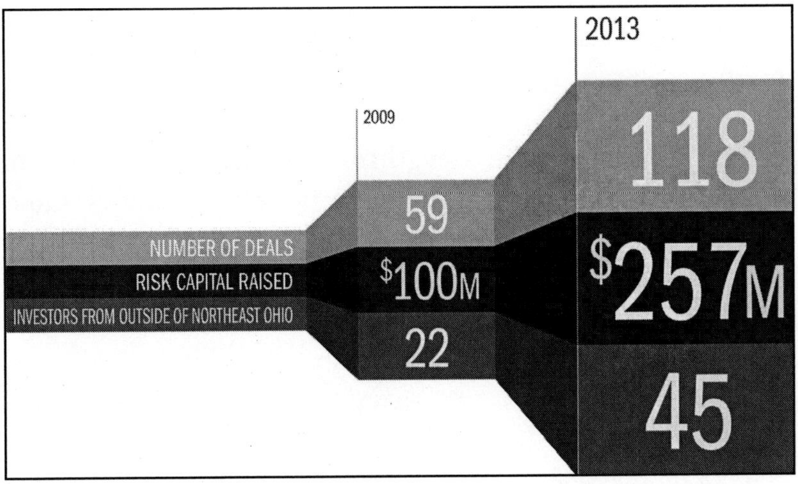

Figure 1

With support from the Ohio Third Frontier, Northeast Ohio has also been able to grow and strengthen the entrepreneurial ecosystem across its twenty-one counties by developing a collaborative network of entrepreneurial support organizations called the JumpStart Entrepreneurial Network. Each organization in the Network fills a specific resource gap, contributing to a comprehensive continuum of support, ensuring all entrepreneurs in the region find the space, capital, advice, and connections they need. This continuum is creating the foundation of an inclusive entrepreneurial ecosystem, where minority, inner-city, and women entrepreneurs are more fully immersed.

JumpStart has also applied the experience and expertise it has gained growing resources and leading Northeast Ohio's entrepreneurial ecosystem in other regions across the country. The model it crafted was noted by the administration of President Barack Obama in 2011 and inspired a national effort called JumpStart America, which now operates as JumpStart. JumpStart's regional projects are fundamentally based on collaboration and partnerships, with the ultimate goal of accelerating entrepreneurial successes and economic outcomes at the regional level. JumpStart has worked with nearly twenty regions across the country.

JumpStart collaborates with each region's existing entrepreneurs, investors, government leaders, philanthropists, and economic development professionals. These community leaders and JumpStart work together to assess regional strengths and weaknesses, identify areas of opportunity and develop implementation plans to address those opportunities.

Through its work, JumpStart is committed to creating, enforcing, and implementing inclusive best practices to ensure long-term economic competitiveness and sustainability.

Student Power

A region that works together to seed and nurture its entrepreneurs is building its economic future on a solid base and assuring the pipeline for sustained growth is full. In Northeast Ohio, the pipeline is not just for seasoned entrepreneurs and postgraduate professionals. Every May, a new class of leaders emerges from our nation's colleges and universities. As many pursue careers in areas like education, law, and medicine, others take a less traditional route. Driven by innovation, many of today's new graduates seek to establish their own businesses and build them from the ground up. These new and emerging entrepreneurs are not only ambitious individuals; they will ultimately help drive the region's economy.

Home to a vast higher education system that includes twenty-seven accredited colleges and universities, Northeast Ohio is not only preparing students to think entrepreneurially in more traditional careers, but it is also taking steps to train and educate the next generation of entrepreneurs—an area extremely important to our region's continued growth. Eleven Northeast Ohio higher education institutions are part of the Entrepreneurship Education Consortium (EEC), which presents multiple opportunities for area students, including an Entrepreneurship Immersion Week every summer and an annual ideaLabs business plan competition. Michael Goldberg, a visiting assistant professor at the Weatherhead School of Management at Case Western Reserve University, an EEC member, taught a massive open online course (MOOC) on entrepreneurship, for which nearly ten thousand people across the globe registered. And multiple non-college organizations are welcoming to student entrepreneurs—including business accelerator/incubator LaunchHouse or The Beta Space at MAGNET, which offers a range of services and mentoring to support and encourage college-age or graduate entrepreneurs.

One of these ideaLabs participants, EvenPlayingField.com—which analyzes, interprets, and reports sports statistics in an easy to understand ways—placed second overall in the 2012 event. "We learned so much from participating in ideaLabs," says Amanda Mass. "Not just about our business necessarily, but you meet so many people giving you advice. Learning how to innovate and think differently is applicable to working in any company, whether it's a start-up or not."

Another resource available to the next generation of Northeast Ohio entrepreneurs is Blackstone LaunchPad. In 2011, the Blackstone Charitable Foundation and the Burton D. Morgan Foundation partnered to bring this national program—which focused on assisting, encouraging, and mentoring promising student entrepreneurs—to area colleges and universities. Taking part are Baldwin Wallace College, Case Western Reserve University, Kent State University and Lorain County Community College. The basic goal of these Blackstone LaunchPad outposts is to help entrepreneurs transform ideas into viable companies with the potential to create jobs and have positive economic impact.

As colleges and universities throughout Northeast Ohio look to create more opportunities for entrepreneurs, high schools are taking similar steps. For example, the Hawken Entrepreneurship Program at Hawken School in Cleveland, Ohio, allows students to develop an entrepreneur's mind-set via intense hands-on experience. Participants in the program form teams and develop their own businesses from the ground up, while adopting the same kind of analytical rigor and immersive community engagement required of other start-ups. The idea is to get students interested in entrepreneurship—and thinking like a nimble entrepreneur—at a young age, so that they have a firm foundation to build upon in the years to come.

While programs like these are still relatively new, they represent a positive trend taking place in Northeast Ohio and beyond. As our economy continues to grow and diversify, we will need innovative entrepreneurs to establish start-up operations and, in turn, create new jobs.

Not only is Northeast Ohio working to equip the next generation of entrepreneurs with the skills they need, the region has a robust economic development system in place to assist those further along in the entrepreneurial cycle. As noted in this chapter, nonprofit support organizations such as JumpStart provide an array of services to emerging start-ups. Throughout Northeast Ohio, more traditional organizations like Chambers of Commerce often provide programs and services specifically for entrepreneurs. There are also a number of business incubators, such as the Akron Global Business Accelerator. One such incubator took a very unorthodox approach to launching businesses; it actually launched a tech industry in an unlikely place: Youngstown, Ohio.

Incubating an Industry

Founded as a mixed-use incubator in 1995, Youngstown Business Incubator (YBI) shifted its focus a few years ago exclusively to IT start-ups, with a specific focus on business-to-business software solutions. Think of places known for launching young software companies: Boston, San Francisco, Silicon Valley, Austin, and Minneapolis. How long does that list get before Youngstown is noted? Yet YBI's leadership determined a software company can start up anywhere—so why not Youngstown?

In fact, such a refined emphasis means that entrepreneurs receive assistance tailored to their specific needs—whether that's shaping an idea into a marketable product, identifying potential funders, or developing a business plan. Because it focuses on one industry, YBI has what it calls a Managed Cluster. This community of YBI Portfolio Companies shares its expertise, technical skills, and resources—a peer network of incredible support.

A shining example of YBI's impact is a company called Turning Technologies. Youngstown resident Mike Broderick had been working in an industry that was focused on corporate meetings and used early audience-response technology. It was very expensive and needed a skilled technician to operate the equipment. He had an idea for an inexpensive interactive software tool that could get audience input from common PowerPoint presentations. He envisioned his invention being used in a variety of environments and especially in education.

He left his job and tried to launch his idea, knowing that all he needed was a little money. But it was the worst time for even thinking of looking for funding, as he was attempting this during the dot-com bust and right after 9/11. He took a second mortgage on his home and opened up a few new credit cards; meanwhile, his wife went back to work full time. Then, he called on the Youngstown Business Incubator, which took a gamble on the company. In May of 2008, the company moved next door to the newly constructed Taft Technology Center with thirty thousand square feet for additional personnel. With growing international demand, Turning opened its first brick and mortar international office in Amsterdam in 2010, now staffed with a General Manager EMEA (Europe, Middle East and Africa) and several, dedicated sales representatives. As of 2014, Turning is home to over two hundred employees and has delivered more than 6 million ResponseCard clickers to K-12 schools, universities, and businesses worldwide. The company is listed in the *Inc.* 5000. Now, Turner gives back by helping other entrepreneurs within the YBI.

Conclusion

There is no one formula for success when it comes to launching viable companies, but the collaborative approach in place in Northeast Ohio—employing traditional and nontraditional economic development organizations and other public, private, and philanthropic partners—seems to offer the right ingredients. Entrepreneurs looking to hedge their bets would be wise to seek regions that understand their needs, that have put the systems in place to nurture their growth, and that provide ready access to capital, workforce, and business development experts. In increasing numbers, entrepreneurs are finding their success not in Boston, Silicon Valley, or Austin, but in places such as Northeast Ohio.

Acknowledgments

The author gratefully acknowledges the contributions of JumpStart, Inc. and the Regional Marketing Alliance of Northeast Ohio to this work.

Ways Our Country Can Nurture Entrepreneurs

Large companies need to provide what was once called *skunk works* projects. This allowed the entrepreneur to develop and be recognized. Then the opportunity to spin out new companies and technologies can follow with the corporate safety net in place. Of course, once the true entrepreneur has sampled the banquet of personal success, the fostering organization would need to break away from traditional employee practices, and allow the entrepreneur to blossom or they will lose the brightest stars.

—John Lauletta, CEO/CTO, Exacter, Inc. (Columbus)

We are approaching a dangerous level of cultural mediocrity that discourages young people to become productive and inventive. Kids will not go into research or development if this is perceived as being *uncool*. We must educate our people.

—Damir Janigro, Cleveland Clinic Foundation and Cofounder, Flocel, Inc. (Cleveland)

The experience of working in an entrepreneurial environment can be the most beneficial education. I am not convinced that entrepreneurial business programs at the college level can ever give a student a true experience. Additionally, guiding people through balanced team building will bring together members who have a variety of skills and can evaluate technology, market opportunities, and raise capital.

—Lauren Wolf, CEO, AeroClay, Inc. (Cleveland)

Identify talented individuals starting from the elementary school level. But, this should not be done by simple tests, quizzes, or surveys. In my opinion, the current curriculum of the elementary, middle, and high schools are not designed to identify, train, or nourish entrepreneurs. If we changed the structure of the curriculum, students will know the benefits of becoming entrepreneurs by the time they get into college.

—Majid Rashidi, Professor, Cleveland State University

Ways Our Country Can Nurture Entrepreneurs (cont'd.)

I think it is up to parents to help their kids nurture that entrepreneurial spirit when they see it. I think teaching kids about entrepreneurship in high school and college would also help. The role of the entrepreneur is a bit lost when so much of what affects our day is the result of giant corporations. To teach that role will certainly help young people have an appreciation for how entrepreneurs affect society and growth.
—Michael Mariola, Owner, Sustainable Foods, Inc. (Wooster)

The real question is how to make it easier for people who are already inclined to be entrepreneurs succeed. Important factors include access to capital. I personally feel that the elimination of capital gains tax will create a change in the landscape, making it more advantageous to invest in start-ups. Ultimately, that could have the greatest impact.
—Steven Marks, Founder, Main Street Gourmet (Cuyahoga Falls)

I truly believe that focusing our entrepreneurial classes and education toward students is the best way to cultivate entrepreneurs. Holding students' hands while they go through the process of starting a small business for the first time will empower them with the knowledge and confidence to do it for real the next time. Not to mention it will also weed out those would-be entrepreneurs who realize it isn't a right fit for them, saving them valuable time and money by learning this while they're still in school.
—Christopher Clark, CEO, Sunflower Solutions (Shaker Heights)

Young people need to see successful entrepreneurship succeed. They also need to have great encouraging mentors. Lastly, they need to have help in making relationships with those important to the success of their venture.
—D. Kirk Neiswander, Founder, The Entrepreneurs EDGE, Inc. (Independence)

Ways Our Country Can Nurture Entrepreneurs (cont'd.)

We have to continue to build a culture in which people aspire to achieve great things and to push for excellence. If we do not believe our kids can achieve more, they will not. We need to develop and nurture passion within our students. Too often in places that I go, I see people doing their jobs haphazardly, without pride or ownership of what they are doing. In certain parts of the world, people in all positions of society approach what they do with the attitude that they want to be the best they can in whatever they do.

—Hiroyuki Fujita, President & CEO, Quality Electrodynamics (Mayfield Village)

In my opinion, a person is a product of his or her environment. Upbringing, family chemistry, schooling experiences, mentors—all play a role in developing a person with imagination and vision needed to become an entrepreneur. The entrepreneur is the exception, not the rule. Planting the seed that makes one entrepreneurial begins at an early age.

—Russ Vernon, Retired Chairman, West Point Market (Akron)

From Rust Belt to Tech Belt with Connections

Rebecca Bagley

Northeast Ohio is a place where manufacturing expertise meets innovation, a region that is transitioning from Rust Belt to Tech Belt, a place that is as much bits as it is bolts.

One of Northeast Ohio's biggest strengths is that our R&D resources are located in proximity to our manufacturing assets. It allows us to quickly take ideas from the research lab to the factory floor to the consumer, and it has made the region a leader in industries like biotech, aerospace, logistics, advanced energy, food processing, additive manufacturing, flexible electronics, water technologies, and lighting.

Northeast Ohio is home to manufacturing giants like Rockwell Automation as well as cutting-edge start-ups like Vadxx Energy. The region's tremendous innovation capacity comes to life when these kinds of companies connect.

Unfortunately, they rarely do. Too often large corporations are not aware of the innovation assets that exist in their backyard. At the same time, smaller companies developing groundbreaking technologies often don't have the know-how or resources to capture the imagination of these large corporations.

This is where intermediaries like NorTech can make a difference. Our mission is to strengthen Northeast Ohio's economic vitality by accelerating the pace of innovation in the region. We believe enhancing the region's ability to turn new ideas and technologies into assets that will transform our economy must be an important part of our competitiveness strategy. Our companies must have the tools and resources to do things differently, do things that have never been done before, and understand and take advantage of national innovation trends.

So, how do we give our companies these tools and resources?

The short answer is: by making connections. Companies in Northeast Ohio will solve problems, increase revenues, and create jobs if we connect them to the region's research institutions, supply chain partners, investors, and other resources they are not aware of or don't have access to. These connections don't just happen. They require thoughtful preparation, strong baseline expertise, skilled facilitation, and persistent follow-through.

Intermediaries like NorTech, BioEnterprise, JumpStart, MAGNET, and Team NEO provide these types of services, which can readily be connected to a growth-oriented business development strategy.

Here's an example: Vadxx Energy is one of the region's most promising companies in the waste-to-energy business. It has developed technology that turns plastic waste, like old grocery bags or milk jugs, back into crude oil. For years, Vadxx ran a pilot-scale facility that demonstrated the technology's power. But its real breakthrough came when Vadxx was introduced to Rockwell Automation.

With the help of NorTech and other intermediaries in the region, Vadxx and Rockwell formed a partnership that ultimately led to a multimillion dollar investment by private equity firm Liberation Capital. As a result of that investment, Vadxx was able to award a $15 million contract to Rockwell to engineer, procure, and construct its first plant in Akron.

In order to grow Northeast Ohio's economy, we need to foster more such opportunities for business leaders from diverse industries to come together and exchange innovative ideas. We need to continue to support promising businesses in the region's emerging industries and connect them to our anchor companies.

These connections accelerate the growth of small businesses, increase the innovation capacity of large corporations, and revitalize Northeast Ohio's economy as the region continues its transition from Rust Belt to Tech Belt.

Experiences Finding Outside Funding

Sunflower Solutions has actually been self-funded. It is the definition of a shoestring start-up, as our untraditional business model made the traditional sources of financing uncomfortable. However, we did secure a small grant from the city of Cleveland based on the fact that we kept our manufacturing in the Northeast Ohio area.

—Christopher Clark, CEO, Sunflower Solutions (Shaker Heights)

A significant amount of capital was secured through the National Institutes for Health (NIH grant) foundation and through Small Business Research Funding Opportunities (SBIR and STTR grants). However, we are still struggling with investors for one of our two ventures.

—Damir Janigro, Cleveland Clinic Foundation and Cofounder, Flocel, Inc. (Cleveland)

I started with $100,000 and I was able to secure that through friends and family. We became profitable before we ran out of that initial money and haven't had to take on anymore. We have no debt; we have grown through cash flow to where we are today.

—Mike Burkons, Founder, Charitee Golf LLC (Shaker Heights)

The Ohio Third Frontier Program was and still is a wonderful program that synergistically brought the academic and industrial institutions together to have significant impact in economic development. This idea of transparent conductive film development is a direct product of such funding. One of the amazing unintended (or maybe intended) consequences of such a program is to bring industrial folks into the same room with academic folks and have them start conversations. This leads to gaining trust, which in turn spawns new opportunities. All other states are envious of our Third Frontier Program—I hear they are studying it intensely.

—Miko Cakmak, Professor, The University of Akron

Experiences Finding Outside Funding (cont'd.)

To get started, we did need to raise some working capital. We went to successful entrepreneurs who knew our work and believed in what we were trying to accomplish. As it turned out, we have not touched a dime of the money we raised since we were fortunate enough to have enough companies prepay for our services—moneys that allowed us to hire a staff and get moving.

—D. Kirk Neiswander, Founder, The Entrepreneurs EDGE, Inc. (Independence)

Raising capital is very difficult: our business is particularly challenging because we are in a very capital-intensive business. The past few years especially have been very difficult economic climates for raising capital and, having been through it, I've concluded that getting people to give you money is probably one of the most difficult things you can try to do in life. Making a case to investors has been well documented and all I can say is that if you are going to be an entrepreneur, you will need a lot of skill in this very difficult task.

—Neil Sater, Cofounder, GreenField Solar (Oberlin)

In the early days, we used credit card advances as a tool because we were unable to obtain funds in addition to our initial borrowings. During this time we were never able to borrow money without having success and always needed a borrowing base that supported the loan. Therefore, our ability to borrow under these circumstances was fairly straightforward.

—Steven Marks, Founder, Main Street Gourmet (Cuyahoga Falls)

We decided not to bring in outside investors since we recognized that this program would require a significant amount of time and most inventors are looking at the exit before entering anything, contrary to the long-term goals that we had set for ourselves and our business

—Bahman Taheri, CEO, AlphaMicron, Inc. (Kent)

Experiences Finding Outside Funding (cont'd.)

By the time we were ready to expand in 1986, three banks were courting us for our business. Unfortunately, banks have tightened their lending requirements today—which is choking small business. The bank we had been in a healthy relationship with for years suddenly became uncomfortable with our business model and size; they required us to seek another bank. We were able to find another bank that believed in us and provided funding to continue building our business.
—Russ Vernon, Retired Chairman, West Point Market (Akron)

Part II

Innovators at Work

Conversations

Impacting Akron, Northeast Ohio, and the United States

Luis Proenza

Dr. Luis Proenza has been involved in national science and technology policy since the 1970s, when he was appointed Study Director of the National Research Council—National Academy of Sciences' Committee on Vision. Additionally, he has served as a member of many other professional, scholarly, and honorary organizations. A recipient of numerous awards and honors, he also has written publications for nationally and internationally recognized journals, edited, and coedited two books, and often is quoted on issues in education, research, economic development, and science and technology policy. As one of the most influential leaders in the region, he is a powerful innovator. His motivation lies in a desire to advance the common good through collaborative networking and building new frameworks to enhance the region's innovation ecosystem.

Proenza's success in marshaling disparate groups into functioning partnerships may be rooted in a lifetime of crossing borders, whether cultural, geographic or conceptual, in pursuit of innovation. His father was born in Cuba, but lived for a time in the US and eventually moved to Mexico, where he partnered with his wife, Proenza's mother, in various business ventures involving silver jewelry. The senior Proenza was determined that his son would think broadly and internationally, and young Luis' travels began at the age of four. He began studying English in first grade, and by the time he was eleven, it was decided his formal education should continue in the US—but where?

"My father feared that if I went too far north I might be too cold; whereas if I went too far south or southwest, I might find so much Spanish-speaking influence, I might never learn English!

And so, after perusing the catalogues of many schools in the Southeast, we settled on Riverside Military Academy in Gainesville, Ga., which was to become a foundational experience for leadership."

After completing his studies at Riverside, Proenza earned a BA from Emory University in 1965, and then went on to study at The Ohio State University and at the University of Minnesota, where he earned his MA in 1966 and his PhD in 1971, respectively. That same year, he joined the faculty at the University of Georgia and began research in retinal neurophysiology. In 1987, he became Vice Chancellor for Research and the Dean of the Graduate School (and later, the Vice President for Academic Affairs and Research) at the University of Alaska. Then, in 1994, he accepted a position as the Vice President for Research and Dean of the Graduate School at Purdue University.

His educational and research career, with international work as varied as the halls of Europe to the ice fields of the Arctic and Antarctic, quickly earned notice. In 2001, then-president George W. Bush named Proenza to the President's Council of Advisors on Science and Technology (PCAST), the nation's highest-level policy advisory group for science and technology. Proenza served as cochair of PCAST's committee on Public-Private Partnerships, and worked on panels for US Research and Development Investments, Technology Transfer, Alternative Energy, Energy Efficiency and Advanced Manufacturing, Personalized Medicine, Information Technology, and Nanotechnology. In 2004, the Secretary of Energy appointed Proenza chairman of the Science and Mathematics Education Task Force and, later, to the Secretary of Energy Advisory Board.

He continues to work at the national level, receiving in 2012 an appointment from the National Academies to its Board on Science, Technology and Economic Policy (STEP). He also serves on the Council of the Government-University-Industry Research Roundtable (GUIRR) of the National Academies. He also is a member of the Council on Foreign Relations and a board member of the State's Science and Technology Institute. Proenza also serves on the executive committee for the Council on Competitiveness, its Manufacturing Competitiveness Steering Committee, and chairs its Regional Leadership Institute Steering Committee.

Throughout his career, Proenza has ardently advocated that entrepreneurs at every level, from individuals launching small businesses to change agents within corporations, government and higher education, must be willing to embrace innovation, disruption, and risk. He firmly believes that "People—and organizations—must adapt to change. Risk is out there and it must be understood." For example, Proenza recommends the process of "open innovation" in which organizations look beyond their own resources to engage external partners and options to leverage existing technologies. Companies like Procter & Gamble and Nike have endorsed the concept, and The University of Akron has gained national attention for its open innovation agreement with international steel products manufacturer, Timken Company. That arrangement was highlighted in a 2013 national report by MIT researchers on innovation and production in manufacturing.

Such innovative approaches have dramatically raised the university's reputation. Within Proenza's first twelve years as president, UA's revenue and research portfolio more than doubled and private donations increased to all-time record highs. Under his leadership, the university has transformed into a powerful engine for regional economic development and collaborative initiatives. His work has distinguished the university nationally and internationally, making UA a recognized national model for technology commercialization, economic development, and corporate-community partnerships.

Two of his most notable accomplishments are the creation of the New Landscape for Learning and New Landscape for Living projects. One of these, the New Landscape for Living, gave rise to the University Park Alliance which is working to revitalize a fifty-block area surrounding UA's campus. To date, the project has produced $300 million in investments to the neighborhood and downtown areas adjacent to campus. Through the New Landscape for Learning, the university financed $620 million in capital construction, which resulted in 22 new facilities, 18 major renovations and additions, and the addition of thirty-four acres of new green space. Proenza's leadership of these efforts has transformed The University of Akron into one of the most attractive metropolitan campuses in the nation.

Proenza insists that universities must serve as conveners and developers for economic development and has propelled his institution into just that role in Northeast Ohio. In a speech entitled "The Power of the Energy of Innovation," originally given on May 14, 2012, Proenza discussed the importance of innovation in the United States and, more specifically, in the greater Akron area. He noted that the competitive nature and success of Americans has long been the envy of other nations, but "at the dawn of the twenty-first century, we find that the primacy that the United States has long enjoyed around the world is increasingly being challenged by the very same forces of technological innovation that America itself unleashed. Other nations are learning how to play the game." And as he emphasized, these nations play very, very well. To understand the current economy and job market, Proenza points to that American legacy of competition and its current dilemma in the global arena. He argues that it is fruitless to defend the status quo because the structures of industry are in constant flux. And, quoting Andrew Reamer and his colleagues, Proenza emphasized: "firms are merging, acquiring, leaving, dying, entering, growing, downsizing, outsourcing and spinning off. At a faster and faster pace, the US economy is experiencing the phenomenon the economist Joseph Schumpeter called 'creative destruction…'"

By acknowledging these changes and educating the American people, Proenza believes that current economic problems in the United States can be overcome. In his speech, he advised, "Our politicians would do well to tell the truth about economic growth and encourage displaced workers to acquire new skills for newly created industries—because the old jobs are not coming back! We must resolutely dismiss all calls for protectionism; we must become much better at developing talent and managing the talent supply pipeline; and, we must do what Americans always do best: innovate!" He applauds organizations like the Kauffman Foundation, which he believes are on the right track. The Kauffman Foundation is known as the foundation of entrepreneurship. Proenza urges, "We need to create a culture of innovation."

And he believes that culture can begin here, in Northeast Ohio. He notes that the longtime shift of manufacturing jobs to the South has halted in the last two years. These jobs have been flowing into the Midwest instead. Proenza shares statistics with his audiences that often amaze and encourage them: between the first quarter of 2010 and the fourth quarter of 2011, the Midwest generated a 5.2 percent increase in manufacturing jobs (as compared to a 2.2 percent increase in the South). Manufacturing jobs have increased specifically in metropolitan areas and about 95 percent of these jobs are very high or moderately high technology jobs. This means that the best kind of manufacturing jobs are flowing in the Northeast Ohio region and the surrounding areas. This is emphasized by the fact that in the Akron metropolitan area (which includes Summit and Portage counties), manufacturing makes up 11.7 percent of all jobs—ranking Akron as thirteenth in the nation for manufacturing jobs and nineteenth in the nation for moderately high technological jobs.

He tells audiences, "I believe we can continue to grow a stronger regional economy if we place innovation at the center of our strategy." When asked how this could be accomplished, Proenza notes that the region needs to better support innovation and entrepreneurship. "More benchmarking is needed. We need to change the risk-adverse culture. We need to attract and upgrade the talent pool. And, we need to realize that chambers of commerce are largely obsolete—they focus on company attraction, taking them away from other regions, but they don't focus on talent attraction or on new wealth creation."

He also quotes Alan Kay, a pioneer in the field of computer technology: "The best way to predict the future is to invent it."[23] Proenza agrees, adamantly believing that "the future has always been predicted by the technologies that invented it." He points to the history of America, suggesting America's global economic leadership is directly dependent on the research and commercialization that preceded it. "Nearly every economist agrees that the creation of new technological knowledge through research is our most direct economic avenue for acquiring added value. They understand that when new knowledge is quantified in a market environment, it creates fuller employment, capital formation, growing profits, and surpluses for reinvestment. Put more simply, research begets new companies, which beget new jobs, which beget economic expansions and the creation of new wealth."

His advice to aspiring innovators is simple: "Just innovate."

References

"Alan Kay Educator and Computing Pioneer." *TED Conferences, LLC.* July 18, 2014. http://www.ted.com/speakers/alan_kay.

Get Them to Drink Your Kool-Aid

Andrew Vaeth

Andrew Vaeth has always felt innovation was in his blood. "I may be the first entrepreneur in the family tree, at least for several generations," he explains. "My parents were particularly tolerant of failure—as long as you learned from it—and very insistent about the old fashioned notion that anyone can do anything he or she sets their mind to." Born in Cleveland Heights and raised in Wooster, Ohio, Vaeth never dreamed of punching a clock. He wanted to create his own destiny.

This was made possible while he was away from home, studying at Indiana University (Bloomington) in the 1980s. After failing a math course which was required for graduation—"I hated it," he remembers, "I skipped this class frequently"—he was allowed to take a new experimental class to fulfill the requirement and graduate on time. The class was on object-oriented software programming. Vaeth was immediately in love with the subject; he has been developing software solutions ever since.

From the beginning, Andrew Vaeth was not afraid of failure. "Entrepreneurs have to steel themselves against failure or they will likely never succeed," he advises. He has had his share of big and small failures and knows that failure can come even after success.

He considers entrepreneurship grueling work, with the biggest hurdles being money and talent. "It is a never-ending battle of having enough cash and attracting (and keeping) the best talent," he insists. Vaeth overcomes these issues by being able to consistently articulate his vision and lead his teams. "I am relentlessly, continually, tirelessly pitching my idea to investors," he admits. Even more, he is an active networker and, because internet software ventures are dependent on outside capital, he is constantly working to attract new sources of funding. He has learned that raising capital is an endless process rather than a discrete event.

These skills have enabled Vaeth to become a respected pioneer in web services and on-demand technologies. He has repeatedly guided his organizations to market success with multiple world-class workforce software solutions. For example, one of his first major successes was ExpenseWire, a company which achieved significant recognition as a high growth, emerging leader in the expense management software space. Here, Vaeth worked on developing solutions for an existing market. He served as president and chief executive officer of ExpenseWire until it was purchased by a Silicon Valley company in 2008.

His latest venture, on the other hand, has allowed him to experiment with building products that will attempt to solve problems in the market that no one else has attempted to solve technologically. This innovative step is known as Cureo and was incorporated in 2009 (originally under the name OptixConnect, LLC). Based in his hometown, Wooster, Ohio, the company develops a social network for private businesses and their stakeholders. Its primary purpose is to design solutions that make it easier for business professionals to interact, be introduced to, communicate with, and share strategic information with investors, board members, advisors, executives, and other VIPs.

Unfortunately, Vaeth does not have a specific formula or process for his success. He simply finds that ideas present themselves anywhere, anytime. However, if he ever finds that his team needs to innovate to solve a problem or if ideas need to be forced to the surface, he brings his team together. "We will collaborate on whiteboards behind closed doors, no phones, no interruptions. If you have a good team, it always works," he insists. He also recommends risk taking. Though he acknowledges it as part of the job, it can be hard. He admits, "In a macro sense, when it comes to considering risking your family's money or the money of outside investors, there is definitely noticeable, underlying pressure influencing just about everything I do."

When it comes to innovation in the United States, Andrew Vaeth cannot understand why entrepreneurship is a sideshow in the national education curriculum. The global economy is fiercely competitive and Vaeth feels, "Entrepreneurship should be sewn into the fabric at an early age—entrepreneurship as an attitude, as a method of approaching new ideas and challenges, as a new kind of work ethic. Our first challenge is getting adults charged with preparing our children to compete in this global workforce. They won't all strike out on their own to create new businesses, but they will have the foundation for innovation, creativity, and growth-through-failure that will propel our competitive success as a nation."

In the Northeast Ohio region, more specifically, Vaeth sees a number of good people and organizations working to support innovation. However, there are problems here, too. Not enough is being done. Vaeth feels the area needs more successful start-ups who will produce new entrepreneurs, new money, and a culture of success. He also feels that, because the talent pool is too shallow in Northeast Ohio, the region needs to attract more design and engineering talent as well as attract more existing, large technology companies which can open branch offices in the area. These two efforts could immediately impact the creative culture and talent pool of Ohio.

For those who aspire to be innovators or who are beginning their ventures, he advises, "Don't be discouraged by those who cannot seem to understand your vision. Be passionate and articulate. Surround yourself with the best people you can find—and get them to drink your Kool-Aid."

The Pursuit of Knowledge Has No End

Charis Eng

When the Cleveland Clinic opened in the early twentieth century, Dr. William J. Mayo called the event an "epoch making step in American medical progress." He went on to indicate this opening recognized that the case of a sick person in this and future generations depended on education and research because the real job of the medical profession was to extend knowledge of what medicine was doing and could do. The clinic was envisioned as a place where all systems of alleviating or curing human maladies would be given impartial, scientific analysis.

Charis Eng grew up in Singapore, surrounded by a family of academics. Three years after moving to Chicago, Illinois with her parents, her father had completed his PhD in the social sciences and wanted to move the family back. But Eng decided to stay in her adopted country. At the age of sixteen, she entered the University of Chicago. She went on to earn her PhD and MD from Chicago's Pritzker School of Medicine. Today, Eng describes herself as a physician-scientist. Such a combination has changed her research process. "The physician half makes clinical observations and the scientist half brings the clinical observation into the lab as a hypothesis," she explains. "My days are filled with the search for evidence, for truly factual knowledge, and then that knowledge pushes me to find more evidence. This is the nature of the beast: we are on a constant journey for knowledge."

Having discovered a passion for genetics around the age of four, Eng has focused her career on cancer genomic research. She is currently the chairperson and director of the Cleveland Clinic's Genomic Medicine Institute and a professor and vice chairperson of the Department of Genetics at Case Western Reserve University. She admits that the reputation of the Clinic is unsurpassed, but admits there are challenges to future growth. The area's decrease in population has consequently shrunk the talent pool. She believes local talent must be stimulated to ensure innovation and entrepreneurship. Eng has faith that Northeast Ohio could be a leader for the rest of the country, as well as the world, if the local talent would collaborate and put aside political and selfish goals.

These ideals stem from her faith in the purity of good science and good medicine. As an altruist who embraces the concept of primum non nocere, "above all, do no harm," Eng has experienced entrepreneurial arenas filled with individuals who only want to stroke their own egos or who are driven purely by financial gains. These individuals lack passion and are, ultimately, unsuccessful. Eng prefers to focus on enhancing the lives of her patients and colleagues, to advance knowledge for the greater good. Her only goal is to speed scientific findings into clinical settings.

If you ask Eng about failure, she will tell you she follows Thomas Edison's maxim: "I have not failed; I've just found 10,000 ways that don't work." Eng insists the scientific process is not bound by success or failure; every discovery leads to a new hypothesis. Though some view hypotheses as failures, she prefers an open-minded approach. Eng advocates that the pursuit of knowledge does not have an endpoint and every endeavor has an accompanying risk factor—but the largest payoffs often come from risk and intuition. She has experienced this process firsthand. When she was a new assistant professor, Eng had few resources. Her competitors included a very well established lab, led by one of the pioneers of human cancer genetics, and a large, commercial-research entity.

"I wanted to find the gene for Cowden Syndrome, which confers a danger of growths in (and on) all parts of the body and confers a high chance of breast, thyroid, and other cancers. If I failed, I would be out of a job," Eng explains. "I found PTEN, one of the body's many tumor suppressor genes. Many people with Cowden Syndrome have been found to have PTEN gene mutations. I was forced to risk my livelihood, but was convinced I would succeed."

This is only the first of many risks Eng took throughout her career. When she accepted the chairperson position at the Cleveland Clinic, Eng led a disruption of the traditional genetic medicine practices (which had been in place since around the 1960s). There was uproar amongst her new colleagues, but Eng was intent to provide her patients in Northeast Ohio access to the advances in genetic medicine. Again, her risk paid off; the Cleveland Clinic Genomic Medicine Institute is recognized as a leader in the practice of genetic medicine and is often asked by other institutions to share their practice model.

Eng's determination is reflected in her advice to aspiring innovators interested in the health industry. She suggests, "Practice good science and good medicine." Yet, Eng believes the definition of entrepreneurs should be broadened to include researchers who are working across disciplines and advises that all innovators must maintain their integrity and view their work through a larger lens. Above all else, young academics must be passionate in their pursuits.

Sources of Motivation

General interest in how the brain works, which turned into why does it stop working as it should? And then, what can we do to fix it?
—Damir Janigro, Cleveland Clinic Foundation and Cofounder, Flocel, Inc. (Cleveland)

I became truly passionate about what Sunflower Solutions does when I had the opportunity to install our prototype solar power system in the field. I traveled to Kenya and worked with Cornell University students to bring power to a primary school that is located in an area where the nearest electricity was a least an hour walk away. During the process and for the several years since then, I have had the extreme pleasure of staying in contact with the school, students, and villagers who use that electricity every day. It was that life-changing moment when I first realized how huge the impact for them was.
—Christopher Clark, CEO, Sunflower Solutions (Shaker Heights)

My motivation to work in the field and start my own company was to solve a problem that I knew existed and was not being addressed.
—John Lauletta, CEO/CTO, Exacter, Inc. (Columbus)

I have always loved the experience of taking care of guests, perhaps even bettering their days, by making food in a restaurant. There is also a lot of room for advancement in the restaurant business, so I stuck with it clear to the ownership position—which agreed with me.
—Michael Mariola, Owner, Sustainable Foods, Inc. (Wooster)

The numerous possibilities in my field totally motivated and energized me since, in the history of industrial development, they have not happened to this degree very often.
—Miko Cakmak, Professor, The University of Akron

Sources of Motivation (cont'd.)

The museum field offers the ability to be engaged in an intellectual and aesthetic activity—which is what I love most—while also offering the possibility of changing public perception and enriching lives. As a person, I feel the need to do something that has a social impact and that is not simply for my own enjoyment and professional development.
—Mitchell Kahan, Director Emeritus, Akron Art Museum

I worked in the family business from my early years through high school and college and fell in love with the business of business, the food industry, and marketing. With my background, I felt I had a skill in taking care of our customers and leading our 165 employees. My passion for the business drove me.
—Russ Vernon, Retired Chairman, West Point Market (Akron)

I wanted to control my own destiny. I didn't like the typical corporate settings where power and control were evident; I hated how I was sometimes treated by people who were power hungry and who didn't care about the people they hurt in the process.
—Steven Marks, Founder, Main Street Gourmet (Cuyahoga Falls)

In the 1980s, I failed my college math course required for graduation. I hated it and skipped this class frequently. In order to make up for the failure, I was approved to take a new experimental class on object-oriented software programming. I loved it, earned my required math credit, and have been inventing software solutions ever since.
—Andrew Vaeth, Founder, Cureo (Wooster)

I wanted to use my science for the public good, not just generating papers.
—Judit E Puskas, Professor, The University of Akron

Be Aware of the Changing Market

Bahman Taheri

"I wanted to create something that was not there before." That was Bahman Taheri's primary motivation for teaming up with Tamas Kosa and Peter Palffy-Muhoray in 1996. That was the year in which the trio founded AlphaMicron (AMI) through the Kent State University Liquid Crystal Institute. The venture was based on liquid crystal science and technology—a science which the American government had, until then, thought impossible. However, AlphaMicron was able to overcome the technical obstacles because of the trio's background as liquid crystal scientists. The company immediately gained funding from the United States Department of Defense, through SBIR awards, and has since performed research and development for the department.

AlphaMicron's first major project was to create an electronically controllable tint technology for Air Force fighter pilots. The company was able to develop a liquid crystal visor that provides electronic tint (known commercially as e-Tint) on demand. Nothing else like this exists in the world. This technology allows men and women in various branches of the Armed Forces to change their protective eyewear in changing battlegrounds and environments. AMI is currently using its technology to create products for mainstream consumers, including ski goggles for snow sports, mirrors for automobiles, visors for motorsports, and for windows.

Through all of this research and development, Taheri has noticed that the clichés are many times true: "necessity is the mother of invention; see a need, fill a need; high risk, high gain." These mantras have helped him generate new ideas and take risks. And though he finds a solution waiting for a question interesting, he knows such situations do not sustain business. So, Taheri's strategy at AMI is to always begin by looking at a need and working towards creating a solution for it.

This strategy has proven to be successful time and time again. Yet, no matter how easily production comes, Taheri admits he was not prepared for the realities of commercialization: "Manufacturing is hard and it is a completely different mind-set than research." He points out, "You have to worry about yield and consumer interactions." He credits AMI's success and ability to overcome these worries to the company's nimbleness. AMI is aware of the need to constantly change—by bringing in new talent, by finding new ways to penetrate the market, by being aware of the changing market terrain—and this skill allows them to thrive.

Such skills have allowed the company to bypass failure, without having to take on outside investors. This has allowed Taheri and his company to set long-term goals for themselves, rather than short-term goals which would be purely for the benefit of the investors. Today, AMI is close to achieving those goals—and setting new ones.

Taheri credits this drive and resulting success to his immigrant background. "Immigrants are entrepreneurs already. They left a country and home to pursue a better life for themselves and their families," he notes. "Immigrants recognize the fact that opportunity is not something that is around forever and, as such, they grab it as hard as they can." He believes that allowing more immigrants into the United States to pursue their entrepreneurial dreams will enable innovation to grow throughout the country.

In Northeast Ohio specifically, Taheri believes the region must recruit small businesses rather than large ones. Though bringing in big corporations allows an instant influx of new jobs, it is a much larger risk because the company could take them away just as quickly—which could devastate an already fragile region. In comparison, Taheri points out, "A small business owner has the greatest amount of skin in the game. We must give small companies an incentive to start business here—we should utilize loans, grants, and in-state tuition for out of state students to spawn growth locally." This would allow new innovators to take root in the region.

To these up-and-comers, Taheri wishes to share the definition of entrepreneurship which one of his professors at Harvard Business School gave him: "Entrepreneurship is a relentless, not reckless, pursuit of a goal without regards to resources currently available."

Views on Failure

It is the failures that create the success. It is a bit of a yin-yang environment when you create a business. Without failure or the threat of failure, you diminish the opportunity to succeed.
—John Lauletta, CEO/CTO, Exacter, Inc. (Columbus)

Failure usually precedes success. The challenge is to learn from failures and to try not to repeat them.
—Majid Rashidi, Professor, Cleveland State University

I try to never look on decisions with regret. If I am teaching a cooking class, I always tell my students that I fully expect to ruin a recipe the first time I make it. By the second time, though, I usually know what the pitfalls are and try to avoid them. In business, I try to surround myself with people who have much more experience than I have and who can help me avoid mistakes. Failure is relative, but for me, there will always be failures at times. But that's fine; I can learn from them.
—Michael Mariola, Owner, Sustainable Foods, Inc. (Wooster)

I have been fortunate in having never experienced failure in my professional career. But, that is not to say there haven't been disappointments. Having any level of ambition means there will be many disappointments because things do not materialize as planned. That is not something to worry about too much, as missing a goal leads to setting new ones that will be achieved.
—Mitchell Kahan, Director Emeritus, Akron Art Museum

Entrepreneurs have to steel themselves against failure or they will likely never succeed. This includes the prospects of failing after success as well.
—Andrew Vaeth, Founder, Cureo (Wooster)

Views on Failure (cont'd.)

Accumulatively, I call failure "experience." Each failure is a wonderful opportunity to learn.
—Miko Cakmak, Professor, The University of Akron

If you can't deal with failure, don't try to be an entrepreneur. One of the primary components of an entrepreneurial mind-set is the ability to face failure, deal with it, and continue on. It takes tremendous tenacity and a lot of people don't have that level of tenacity.
—Neil Sater, Cofounder, GreenField Solar (Oberlin)

I don't even use the word failure. There may have been some things along the way that have not gone exactly the way I thought they would, however I consider the process of redirecting efforts toward a successful outcome just something one does. I do things until they become successful—thus, no failure.
—Hiroyuki Fujita, President & CEO, Quality Electrodynamics (Mayfield Village)

We just kept trying new processes—discarding the failed ones and keeping what was working. What we found was that small business owners were too busy to actively manage campaigns even if they understood social media so we focused on building a program that focused on solving one of the key issues: time. Shifting our focus here has set our company apart from the rest of our competition.
—Shon Christy, Founder, Christy Creative (Akron)

Thoughts on Akron and Akron-Initiated Innovation

George R. Newkome

I am an Akronite, as were my parents, and I grew up in a time when money was in short supply. It was critical to be inventive and to try "it," whatever "it" might be, and to learn from those experiments and experiences. When the radio died, I took it apart and tried to repair it. Usually a tube burned out—much like replacing a light bulb—and I walked to the local radio store for a new one. I plugged in the replacement tube and generally the radio came to life. When the motor in the car burned more oil than gas, I pulled the engine out of the car with a neighbor's block and tackle, looked for things that were loose, replaced them, put it all back together, and with a little luck, it would run. Mistakenly, I assumed that all of those leftover parts were unnecessary. It was experiences such as these that one learned to ascertain what was important, and who had the items that could be borrowed and then returned at no added costs. One learned to be resourceful. After all, if you did not personally try things, how could you learn how to take a chance?

In those early days, I cannot emphasize the importance of the Boy Scouts in the areas of leadership, survival, friendships, adventure, and innovation. In essence, attaining the rank of Eagle Scout was an accomplishment that could not be taken away. The Boy Scout law leads to the conclusion that a person must be trustworthy, loyal, helpful, friendly, courteous, kind, obedient, cheerful, thrifty, brave, clean, and reverent; words to live by throughout life.

On the other hand, ideas occur for a variety of reasons. As we accumulate facts, one can effectively learn not to waste time on things that are easily acquired by simply asking. They are also derived from the interactions that we have and the observations that we make with the people we meet throughout our lives. Thus, people trying to solve problems need to eliminate the simple things, look around for the obvious, and then put it out of mind until the solution becomes apparent by new observations.

This leads us to the first of several conclusions: life is a pinball machine! One knows the number of pinballs available, where the ball starts, and where it (they or we) will end up, *but* it is all of the interactions (bumpers, individuals, or neighbors) that the ball comes in contact with that are critical to solving any problem. It is all very serendipitous, except for the flippers that you control. You'll get a better idea of exactly what I mean as we go on.

I have never thought of myself as an entrepreneur; rather, I have always felt entrepreneurial. I listen to what other people need and try to connect them to what they need or want. At times, the solution appears obvious, but not to those who cannot see the connection. For better or for worse, they did not bump into the same things that I did. The key, of course, is to aspire to a long career (and life!), never forget to store the facts, and then try to retrieve them at the appropriate moment. Thus the longer that you are in the game, the better the odds are of solving the problem!

I also believe that the ability to read, combined with an understanding of mathematics, and an eye for the arts are critical to being able to see the tree in the forest. For instance, shapes have been an essential part of my life for the last three decades. As an organic chemist, I wondered, "Can one make macromolecules possessing tree-like shapes?" The answer is, of course, yes. But it was the architectural picture of a tree that triggered my mind to connect that shape into an ordered nanoscopic structure, which then led to new, highly branched organic molecules. This has subsequently become the platform for many creative scientists and engineers to expand this basic concept into an entire new discipline within polymer science.

So, we know that resourcefulness, ideas, interactions, and knowledge all play a role in the formation of an entrepreneur. Now the question remains, "How does one train an individual to become entrepreneurial or innovative?" A simple answer is to try to teach it in a college of business at a local university. However, I would argue that one cannot teach a person to be an entrepreneur, since each individual has different likes and dislikes. Every person is unique, and cannot be melded into someone that he or she is not desirous of being. One can be taught the principles of innovation, if there are any, but each individual, much like a pinball, must be willing to be pushed around by a lot of clever, innovative people, who can, with time, rub off a small part of their uniqueness. Being receptive to the positives and negatives of others is not a given; however, one must be willing to accept the input and be willing to tailor it to their own image and likeness. It must then be aged so that it truly is an acceptable and comfortable lifestyle, with personal modifications, for the rest of their lives. They are then obliged to pass their knowledge on to the next pinball or person travelling the gauntlet. In essence, with time, they will be a positive bumper for the next generation.

Helping others to start their own business has been a large part of my life for the past quarter century. My colleagues and I have helped others to create over 120 companies. During my time at the University of South Florida in Tampa, everyone was moving from the Rust Belt to the Sunbelt so the growth in Florida was easy and, in essence, all downhill. Akron, Ohio, however, was not as sure a thing. Upon my return to Akron, the biggest questions on my mind were, "Can one create a model where Northeast Ohio would be a home for the innovative spirit?" and "Can one retain the wisest and brightest in Akron?" Akron was good to me in those early years, and my hope was to return some of the business growth back to my hometown. So, with these challenges before me, President Proenza attracted me from Florida back to Akron—from a warm and sunny climate to several feet of snow and subzero weather! Years later, my questions have all been answered in the affirmative. Thanks to my colleagues, we have actually altered the business climate from ultra-conservative to a more moderate "let's try it" attitude. In a few months, we will have started our 50th company in Akron. The ARCHAngel's network is over six hundred individuals, and the 80+ companies that have presented to this network have raised more than $160 million—not bad for a decade of work from a group of selfless individuals, who have been superb bumpers to the communities of greater Northeast Ohio.[24] As life rolls on, the seeds of innovation have been planted and watered, and Northeast Ohio is actually turning into a marvelous environment with a large supply of fresh water, warmer winters, no fear of rising oceans, a three hundred year supply of natural gas, and a group of wonderful Americans.

Little did I know that a Kent State graduate could go so far. After a few months at Firestone, even though I earned a great salary, I quit to return to a new PhD program in chemistry at Kent and became one of their first graduates. Without the guts to try something that I really loved, I would have been out of a job, along with many others, when Firestone stopped tire production in Akron. One must follow their instincts, or at least probe the edges, before taking the leap. We are expected to play the game until the last pinball has been played. Who knows, there may be more fun as one grows from being the pinball in action to the bumper, or person, who is trying to help the next generation. Life rolls on!

Advice is cheap, but there is always a fifty-fifty chance that it will help someone else. So, if I have to give advice, I leave you with this: One needs to have a good time, enjoy what you do, and always try to help your fellow man (and woman). Someday that last pinball will be played and as it drops into the hole, please remember that all of your actions have been instilled in all of those bumpers and flippers in that pinball machine of life, just as theirs were instilled in yours.

The next generation will be using your imbedded knowledge, absorbed by your actions, to better themselves. Strive to leave a positive, unselfish legacy by pushing people up so that future entrepreneurs can succeed and be innovative. As such, generations will roll on and you will forever continue to be part of the future.

Value Interaction

D. Kirk Neiswander

Growing up in Northeast Ohio, D. Kirk Neiswander gained business experience at an early age—on a paper route. "I also learned the value of a dollar by having to go out and earn it by washing cars, cutting grass, raking leaves, shoveling snow, and doing odd jobs," he remembers. "I learned responsibility (in any kind of weather) and how to provide a good service. I learned about buying and selling." Neiswander attended Denison University, where he earned a BA in Mathematics and Economics. His interest in business eventually led him to the Weatherhead School of Management, Case Western Reserve University where he earned his MBA in General Management. At Weatherhead, he did not focus on any specific area of concentration but instead pursued a little of everything which he thought would better prepare him to eventually run his own business. He had always planned to settle in Northeast Ohio, insisting, "I somehow acquired this passion for entrepreneurship and innovation and I could see its impact on our regional economy. Having grown up in Northeast Ohio, I wanted to see if I could put these interests and accumulated skills to good use by helping this region grow and prosper."

In 1983, Neiswander created the Entrepreneurial programs at his alma mater, the Weatherhead School of Management. In 1986, he became an officer of Enterprise Development, Inc. which was a separate nonprofit organization that eventually became a part of CWRU. He stayed at Case Western Reserve for over twenty-two years, creating new courses, conferences, retreats, breakfast series, recognition events, networking events, and specialized services for entrepreneurs and midmarket companies. He came to realize and believe that anyone running their business is likely to be more productive and highly efficient no matter what the business.

Like his father, an architect who ran his own company, Neiswander had the opportunity in 2005 to create a new organization that could implement some of his new ideas. Because he had experience running a nonprofit organization and had a strong understanding of business, he was in a unique position. He founded and became the president of the Entrepreneurs EDGE, a 501c3 nonprofit organization which fosters entrepreneurship, innovation, and economic development in Northeast Ohio. This new company focused on growing the value of existing midmarket companies that sell some of their goods and services outside of the northeastern region, allowing fresh capital to infiltrate the market. Neiswander created a metric to measure the value any one midsized company could make to the region. The metric tool works by adding together the individual company's earnings with the total taxable compensation for all their employees working in Northeast Ohio. Neiswander's theory was that the higher the aggregate total for a company, the more that will come back to the community in purchases from other local vendors, taxes to support the infrastructure, and philanthropy to support important civic causes.

The EDGE found immediate success in that many of the initial customers, who had worked with Neiswander before at CWRU, had approached him looking for him to continue creating new products and services. He admits, "Most entrepreneurs have a product or service and need to find customers. I had customers and needed to create a product!" The customer's faith in Neiswander's abilities was probably built on his ability to find innovative ideas anywhere.

He is constantly finding inspiration through his relationships with his customers, his observations of their wants and needs, his strategy of applying good, successful ideas from completely different industries to his own company, as well as his trust in his subconscious, which he allows plenty of time to come to fruition. (He keeps a notebook by his bedside and near the shower, where he gets some of his best ideas.)

Though his company has not struggled financially so far, Neiswander admits there were aspects of the process which were difficult. Government approval for nonprofit status took longer than expected. It was also very difficult to decide where to use EDGE's limited resources in creating new products. He credits his contacts, reputation, creativity, education, and experiences for enabling him and his company to make these difficult decisions. Furthermore, by choosing to commit to a company culture and wait for employees who fit this profile—people who were interested in creating new value with a lot of autonomy and who wanted to listen to customers—enabled him to find great partners and employees.

Of course, there was some risk taking involved. Once EDGE was on solid financial ground, the young company was eager to take bigger risks. "I always try to encourage risk taking with our staff," Neiswander admits. In fact, his past is full of moments when he was able to prove his superiors wrong with new ideas that they did not think would work by spending the needed time on the projects with plenty of creativity. "In most cases, these new ideas did work, allowing us to change the way the game was played and positioning us as a leader as well as a perceived company with creative skills that can deliver. (The programs were also quite profitable!)"

Kirk Neiswander believes that his success can inspire and encourage young innovators. "Young people need to see successful entrepreneurship succeed. They also need to have great encouraging mentors. Lastly, they need to have help in making relationships with those important to the success of their venture," he insists. Neiswander serves as an advisor to a number of smaller growth companies.

He also serves on the advisory board for the MAGNET Innovation programs, was the founding chairman of E City (and still serves on the board of the organization, which merged with Youth Opportunities Unlimited), and is on the board of the McGregor Foundation.

He strongly believes that manufacturing will continue to be an important aspect of Northeast Ohio culture and that the region can take steps to support innovation and entrepreneurship. Northeast Ohio must recognize and reward successful innovation across the "spectrum," which Neiswander explains is a spectrum of success ranging from great promise at the onset to achieving a lifetime of success. By utilizing and rewarding this spectrum, lifetime achievers can act as great mentors to the next generation.

Kirk Neiswander believes that companies in Northeast Ohio are succeeding and becoming quite profitable, but are wary of hiring new employees (due to financial and political uncertainty). Companies are looking for good, innovative employees—but they're having a hard time locating them. He finds that they lack marketing skills, entrepreneurial skills, technical skills, and are simply inexperienced. He encourages young innovators to get involved, to test their concepts. Northeast Ohio companies need lots of innovative thinkers who can make good on implementing their ideas and the region can use all the successful entrepreneurs who choose to reside here.

Views on Risk Taking

"Risk is in every decision. We acknowledge it, then move through analysis, assessment, and, finally, to decision. When the assessment does not result in a clear decision, we make one anyway just to move forward with the process. When we make a wrong decision, we correct it and move forward that way."
—*John M. Finley II, Founder, MemPro Ceramics Corporation (Akron)*

As an entrepreneur, every decision is a high-risk proposition. If an initiative fails, it either costs money or creates a lost opportunity to have done something else. Identifying an impending risk and then engineering a way around it is the best way to mitigate risk.
—*John Lauletta, CEO/CTO, Exacter, Inc. (Columbus)*

Risk is exciting. I like to gamble, but I always play the odds first.
—*Joseph Kennedy, Professor, The University of Akron*

Risk is inherent in any entrepreneurial start-up.
—*Lauren Wolf, CEO, AeroClay, Inc. (Cleveland)*

I prefer to get into situations where I believe the deck is stacked in my favor. Though, for me, risk is the constant reminder of what is at stake, of what can be lost. I can appreciate it for that reason. At the same time, it provides me with a sense that failure is not an option.
—*Michael Mariola, Owner, Sustainable Foods, Inc. (Wooster)*

In a nonprofit, one must always be conscious of maintaining public trust, which means any risk taken must be carefully calibrated and easy to explain. Most importantly, I always have a backup plan if my risky choice fails.
—*Mitchell Kahan, Director Emeritus, Akron Art Museum*

Views on Risk Taking (cont'd.)

Without risk, there will be effectively no progress as far as technological developments are concerned. Someone has a vision and sets about making that vision reality and in the process takes a wide range of risks. Obviously one has to educate oneself to minimize the chances of failure in the process.

—Miko Cakmak, Professor, The University of Akron

The clichés are true: "high risk, high reward." We all understand that to be truly innovative, you need to venture into an area that is largely uncharted—a venture that carries with it a significant risk.

—Bahman Taheri, CEO, AlphaMicron, Inc. (Kent)

Good leaders know that the biggest payoff comes from smart, calculated risks. It is important to point out that after objective review of risks and benefits, the final arbiter is intuition, something many good leaders possess.

—Charis Eng, Founding Chair, Cleveland Clinic Genomic Medicine Institute

Sunflower Solutions, being a recent start-up company, has a large amount of risk in everything it does. Spending our hard-earned revenue on anything requires a lot of planning and thought; in the beginning, personally spending my own savings to start a company based on an unproven idea took a lot of risk. I do not think any entrepreneur can separate him or herself from risk—one can look to reduce the amount of risk, but it is always there.

—Christopher Clark, CEO, Sunflower Solutions (Shaker Heights)

Learn to Improvise for the Public Good

Judit E. Puskas

Educated in Hungary, Dr. Judit Puskas experienced a completely different culture and academic system than her Western colleagues. "Nothing was handed to us—we had to improvise," she remembers. Ultimately, this educational system proved excellent; it made her resourceful, determined, and well-rounded.

Originally interested in polymer research and development in the microelectronic, paint, and rubber industries, Puskas' interests shifted when she began her academic career. She studied at the Technical University of Budapest, Hungary under Professor Ferenc Tüdös, Professor Tibor Kelen, and at The University of Akron under Professor Joseph P. Kennedy. She earned an MESc in 1977 and a PhD in 1985, in organic and biochemical engineering and plastics and rubber technology respectively.

However, only a few years later, Puskas felt a career change was necessary. "I wanted to use my science for the public good, not just generating papers," she admits. In 1996, she began to study green polymer chemistry, biomimetic processes and biomaterials, living and controlled polymerizations, polymerization mechanisms and kinetics, thermoplastic elastomers, polymer structure and property relationships, and probing the polymer-bio interface. Such wide-ranging (and complex) interests have made Puskas well prepared for the technical aspects of her innovative pursuits, but she admits she is weak when it comes to business. Therefore, her entrepreneurial ventures have been as a member of a team, often finding good business men and women to work with.

It was with such a team that she coinvented and patented the polymer used on the TAXUS coronary stent, the Translute Polymer. The stent, which is a device used to reduce Restenois (the narrowing of a blood vessel, restricting blood flow), utilizes Translute's proprietary polymer carrier technology to control the release of drugs, to enable uniform distribution of the drug, and to maintain coating integrity during preparation, delivery, and stent expansion. Without this polymer, the stent could not function safely and effectively. Puskas and her business partners founded spin-off companies that intend to market some of her new polymers.

Puskas sees her venture as a simple answer to a market that is always seeking new medical devices. Yet, she notes: "There is no success without failure. Sometimes we do one hundred unsuccessful experiments before one succeeds." Though her product was highly sought after, she still struggled to find research funding (both federal and private). More importantly, she struggled against gender bias. She described the world of science and technology as "the old boys' network," something difficult to access and a world which she is constantly struggling to penetrate. "It's extremely hard work," she admits.

And she works hard. Not only does she teach and research at The University of Akron, but she is also one of the editors of *WIREs*, an interdisciplinary review of nanomedicine and nanobiotechnology published by Wiley-Blackwell. She also serves as a member of the Advisory Board of the *European Polymer Journal*. She has more than 370 publications, is the inventor or coinventor of thirty-one United States patents and applications, and is involved (as either a chair or organizer) in a number of international conferences. Furthermore, she is the recipient of several awards, including: the Professional Engineers of Ontario, Canada Medal in Research and Development (1999); the Premier's Research Excellence Award (2000); the

Mercator Professorship Award from the Deutschen Forschungsgemeinschaft, German Research Foundation (2004); the LANXESS Industrial Chair (1998–2008); the "Chemistry of Thermoplastic Elastomers" Award of the Rubber Division of the American Chemical Society (2009); and the Woman of Achievement Award. She was also elected a fellow of the American Institute of Medical and Biological Engineering in 2010. That same year, she was awarded her fourth NSF and her first NIH grant—the first in The University of Akron's Department of Polymer Science. After her move to the Department of Chemical and Biomolecular Engineering in 2012, she was one of the five winners of the GE Healthymagination Breast Cancer Challenge Award, selected from four hundred international applications.

She credits many of these accomplishments and awards to risk taking and self motivation. "The fire comes from within," she insists, believing firmly that an individual either has the drive or does not.

However, she notes that problems with innovation are larger than internal drive. There are problems with the education system in the United States, which has been put in place to cultivate entrepreneurs, but is not succeeding as it should. "The system needs to be flexible, to be able to change with the changing environment. I have lived and worked in Hungary, Canada, and the United States—and the US system is still the best. It is critical that we establish a new educational system at the elementary and high school levels. American students are just as bright as students of any other nation, but they do not get the stringent basic education (reading, writing, and math) necessary to develop our future inventors and entrepreneurs."

In the Northeast Ohio region specifically, she feels that more students—especially underrepresented minorities—must be made aware of the resources available and be able to gain access to more materials. Puskas also feels that universities could do more by perhaps offering innovation forums where entrepreneurs could present their ideas directly to venture companies. "There are obstacles," she admits, "but if they throw you out the door, come back through the window. Never give up on your dream."

The Best of Many Cultures

Hiroyuki Fujita

A Japanese national who came to Cleveland in 1992 to study physics at Case Western Reserve University (CWRU), Hiroyuki Fujita now holds fifteen patents, has published more than thirty papers and abstracts, and has received numerous awards from the state, national, and international governments for his excellence in imaging technology and manufacturing.

Fujita finds that both his education and his ability to connect the dots have been major contributors to his success. Studying the sciences trained him to be exact. It also taught him to look at things both broadly and in fine detail. After receiving his PhD in physics in 1998, Fujita served as an adjunct professor of physics and radiology at CWRU and electrical engineering at the University of Queensland in Australia. These positions taught Fujita how to effectively communicate concepts as well as how to motivate others. "I think I have been extremely fortunate in my life to have had the opportunity to travel throughout the world and live in different societies. Through these experiences, I have the benefit of being able to pick what I believe is the best of many cultures and blend them into my vision for my companies," he notes.

He also acknowledges his mentors as sources of inspiration. "The philosophies of Dr. Kazuo Inamori and Albert B. Ratner and their passion for success have served as a key platform for the development of my businesses." Both men taught Fujita the importance of creating a business which would better society and mankind. But, ultimately it was his business education and experience which inspired him to build Quality Electrodynamics. Also known as QED, Fujita's company was founded almost seven years ago in Mayfield Village, Ohio. He serves as both president and CEO, overseeing the research and development, as well as the manufacturing and sales of the company's primary product: state-of-the-art radiofrequency (RF) detectors and coils for magnetic resonance imaging (MRI) scanners.

In 2009, *Forbes* designated QED as one of the "20 Most Promising Companies in America." Then, in 2010, Fujita was awarded the Ernst & Young Entrepreneur of the Year Award. He also was named one of the top entrepreneurs in America by *Inc. Magazine* that year, as well as the following year. *Inc.* also placed QED in the *Inc 500*, calling it one of America's fastest growing companies. Also in 2010, Fujita founded his second company, *e*QED. This solar energy company focuses on the research, development, manufacture, and distribution of highly efficient, cost effective, and reliable microinverters. (Solar microinverters convert a direct current from a single solar panel to an alternating current; they are an alternative to traditional central inverters and are considered more advantageous because shading or panel failure does not disproportionately reduce the output of an entire array of microinverters.) In recognition of growing a successful high-tech manufacturing company in the United States, President Barack Obama and First Lady Michelle Obama invited Fujita to be an honored guest at the 2012 State of the Union Address.

His involvement in the health care and the clean energy industries stem from a motivation to build solutions for the betterment of society and mankind. Adopting the philosophies of his mentors, Fujita aims to build a company which not only produces such solutions, but also gives back to the society in significant and meaningful ways. "I realized through my experience in more established world-class companies that medical technologies truly have the power to change the outcome of people's lives. As I worked within these companies, I constantly thought about how we could build these technologies more efficiently. Not everybody approaches their work with this kind of drive," he acknowledges. "I began to think and dream about building my own company, one in which I would be surrounded by people who also woke up every day with optimism and the drive to make the world a better place."

QED is the actualization of this dream. It all began with Fujita's commitment to two key customers who wanted him to build them much-needed technologies within time frames that they couldn't meet on their own. "I bet everything on my team's ability to execute," he admits. With the help of various grants from the state of Ohio, the Japanese government, the Global Cardiovascular Innovation Center at the Cleveland Clinic, NIH, and others, Fujita and his team were able to succeed. "Once we proved that we could execute on the initial set of technologies promised, we were able to secure ongoing partnerships with our customers that have enabled us to brainstorm more and better solutions for them. We will never relax and assume that these relationships are comfortable—we know that we must continue to execute and innovate. It is a never-ending journey."

Such aggressive and consumer-oriented business practices enabled both QED and *e*QED to begin selling their products more quickly than other early-stage companies—which directly contributed to Fujita's noteworthy success. But, of course, as Fujita explained to Cleveland's *The Plain Dealer* in 2010, "Nothing happens by chance. You have to make it by determination."[25] And, for Fujita's company, determination and practicality often outweigh risk taking. Because he believes too many entrepreneurs build prototype technologies without the proper customer relations, his team mitigates such risks by listening thoroughly to the consumer. These strategic relationships allow the company to provide customers with products truly wanted and needed—which, consequently, makes risk taking unnecessary.

If you ask if he has ever struggled with failure, he'll tell you he doesn't even use the word. In his opinion, things may not always go exactly the way he thought they would but this is only a part of a process towards a successful outcome. "I do things until they become successful—thus, no failure." He insists.

When it comes to the future of innovation, Fujita hopes we continue to build a culture in which people aspire to achieve great things and to push for excellence. "If we do not believe our kids can achieve more, they will not. We need to develop and nurture passion within our students." He advises, adding, "Too often in places that I go, I see people doing their jobs haphazardly, without pride or ownership of what they are doing. In certain parts of the world, people in all positions of society approach what they do with the attitude that they want to be the best they can in whatever they do. These are fundamental attitudes that must exist within our entrepreneurs." He strongly believes that if our society established such attitudes early in life, innovation and entrepreneurship would be a natural outgrowth.

He advises young innovators to aspire to build something for a higher purpose, not just for profit. "Think about building real value for your customers while remaining humble and keeping expenses efficient. The profits will come." Especially for young people with the right attitude and focused effort (because, according to Fujita, it's not all about personal ability). He uses QED as an example; it is currently struggling to fill positions. "My company is currently recruiting its engineers and scientists from around the world, but some of the backgrounds I'm seeking are in short supply globally. Why do we have significant numbers of openings in certain types of positions in this region and thousands of people graduating from our states' institutions each year that cannot fill these positions?" Fujita urges the Northeast Ohio region to fight against this trend, to not settle for these insufficiencies. He believes the region could better support innovation through the continual development of educational programs that encourage entrepreneurship and also build technical skill sets.

"So many people in our community have helped me along the way and have done so, not from the positions in which they work, but from their hearts and their true desire to support my vision," Fujita reveals. "There are so many positive aspects to doing business in Northeast Ohio and this is why I am truly committed to building my global business here."

References

Pledger, Marcia. "CEO of Quality Electrodynamics Sees Teamwork As Key to Tech Start-ups Success." *The Plain Dealer* (Cleveland, OH), June 16, 2010.

Ways to Generate New Ideas

First I understand the ideas in my stomach (intuition), then in my head. They just come to me.

—Joseph Kennedy, Professor, The University of Akron

For culinary development, I am often inspired by products that I find (local, seasonal). I read cookbooks and look at as many menus as I can to look for new ideas. For business, I try to listen to the news and read as many leadership and inspiring business stories as I can.

—Michael Mariola, Owner, Sustainable Foods, Inc. (Wooster)

First there has to be a need, a pull, and this prepares the mind. The key to the development of new ideas is power of preparation and power of observation. Ideas may be there, but one has to have good preparation and be equipped with observation skills to see it.

—Miko Cakmak, Professor, The University of Akron

I often just read or make observations—I come up with ideas to expand on what I learned. Also, I get ideas by coming up with ways to solve problems or make work flow easier.

—Ronald Bucci, Administrative Director, MetroHealth (Cleveland)

As I went through the days and travels that took me across the country and through Europe, I would always be aware of my surroundings in a new city. I would take out the telephone directory and look for businesses similar to mine. I found that ideas are everywhere, every day as you go through your life. So, bottom line, my recorder captured my ideas. Trade shows were a major source of new products. I would always look at a product or idea and see how I could add value making that product or service work for Akron, Ohio.

—Russ Vernon, Retired Chairman, West Point Market (Akron)

Ways to Generate New Ideas (cont'd.)

The process of generating and building upon innovation for me is all about constantly asking the question *Why?* Taking things for granted or assuming that, just because things are being done a certain way, they have to be done that way is the biggest constraint to creativity, idea generation, and innovation.

—Christopher Clark, CEO, Sunflower Solutions (Shaker Heights)

"Ideas present themselves anywhere, anytime. In the normal course of business, if we need to innovate to solve a known problem and force ideas to the surface, we will collaborate on whiteboards behind closed doors, no phones, no interruptions. If you have a good team, it always works."

—Andrew Vaeth, Founder, Cureo (Wooster)

New ideas are the result of a thought process being focused on solving a specific problem. You can't just say "That's not possible"—it's better to say, "Wait a minute, could that be possible?"

—Bernard Sater, Cofounder, GreenField Solar (Oberlin)

Our best ideas come from brainstorming sessions which include individuals with different backgrounds and experiences. Our first rule is always: there is no such thing as a stupid idea. Someone always plays the devil's advocate and it really helps us come out with the best idea.

—Shon Christy, Founder, Christy Creative (Akron)

It Takes Tremendous Tenacity

Bernard and Neil Sater

After a long and successful career as a scientist, inventor, and engineer at NASA Glenn Research Center, Bernard Sater retired early in 1994 and founded PhotoVolt, Inc. His goal was to develop a type of high intensity photovoltaic (PV) concentrator solar cell that would enable solar energy to achieve lower cost per watt than what was possible with the then-current, more conventional technologies. In 2008, PhotoVolt combined with GreenField Steam & Electric Co., and GreenField Solar was born. Based outside of Cleveland, GreenField Solar is currently working to commercialize its technology and move its products into volume production. Bernard's PhotoVolt cell technology is a high performance, low cost, high voltage, low series resistance silicon solar cell which provides near-optimum current collection without sheet resistance, current crowding, or blockage of illumination. Because the cell is more robust and less expensive to produce, it makes power systems economically viable for widespread application and makes the product cost-efficient and competitive in the alternative energy market.

Bernard and Neil Sater are more than father and son—they are the founders and executives of GreenField Solar. Bernard is the Chief Scientist. He earned a BEE degree from The Ohio State University and an MSEE from Cleveland State University. He has been awarded five patents and had taken additional graduate courses at the University of Toledo. Neil, on the other hand, is the businessman and president of the company. He earned a BSEE from The Ohio State University and an MBA in finance and marketing from Wright State University. He has been awarded one patent, spent most of his career in business development management at Intel, worked previously as an engineer for Spectra-Physics (where he was also an Associate Scientific Fellow), and has also taught courses in the MBA program at Myers University. Though Bernard admits their educational backgrounds have helped them both, he also notes, "Neither of us really had an educational foundation in entrepreneurialism. That's been on-the-job training." His son agrees, noting an entrepreneurial mind-set isn't something that can be taught in school.

Neil is the first to admit that he and his father failed before they succeeded. "If you can't deal with failure, don't try to be an entrepreneur," he advised, adding that this was not just for the founders, but for the entire team as well. The ability to face failure is a primary component of an entrepreneurial mind-set—it takes tremendous tenacity and many people don't have it. But, Neil points out, his father does. He often looks to his father as a role model for tenacity.

Yet, even Bernard struggled against barriers as an entrepreneur. "Early on, I was considered an outsider to the existing PV community, which made it difficult to find support for my invention." He stayed focused and continued fighting to demonstrate the commercial viability of his invention, proving that major technical breakthroughs can originate outside the established industry. This tenacity eventually earned him the support of the NASA Glenn Research Center as well as the support of the late Dr. Chandra Goradia, a renowned PV researcher at Cleveland State University. It also led to grants from the United States Department of Energy. Neil notes the importance of such grants, since raising capital in this industry is particularly challenging because it is a capital-intensive business. "Raising money for a technology venture is probably one of the most difficult things you can try to do in life," he admits.

Finding funding was just one aspect of the entrepreneurial world which Neil and Bernard struggled with. When they first began, Neil thought he was ready for the challenges, but it was much more difficult than he could have imagined. Now, he believes it is easy for people to idealize entrepreneurship because of the popular success stories, like Apple or Facebook for example. "When you read the stories about the founder's early days, you think it sounds so quaint and you say 'I have great ideas, I can be the next Steve Jobs,' but what you don't see is that for every success story there are hundreds or thousands of failures. It's a far more daunting task than you'll imagine when you read the success stories," Neil says. The idea is the easy part, he notes—and the failures can occur for even the greatest ideas. He has learned that the hard part, the heavy lifting, comes after the idea: raising funds, building a team, proving your great idea (and then selling it), building a profitable operation, and then scaling up volume to a critical mass. "There will be a million failures along that path," Neil warns. "And after you've hit the first thousand, you'll be ready to quit."

GreenField Solar has had to struggle against all of these barriers. Again, Neil credits tenacity for enabling the team to overcome them. The company continues to grow, but both men know there is a long road ahead. In this economic climate, Neil has noticed that investors don't like risk—a frustrating paradox when it comes to finding funding. So, the company works to minimize both technical and business risks. "From a technology perspective, you have got to do whatever you can do to minimize risk because the road from invention to commercialization is long and very difficult. If you stretch that out too far, you won't be able to get enough capital to fund the process. On the business side, risk should also be minimized. But, you've got to take calculated risks to define your strategic focus and to try to make it happen," Neil advises, stressing that *calculated* is key. In his opinion, taking excessive risks without calculation is a sure path to failure.

In Bernard's experience, it is much more than simply calculating risks: it's generating new ideas, too. He has found that his most innovative ideas come while he is trying to solve real life technical problems. These ideas are not spontaneous; they are a direct result of a focused thought process. "But, I think you've also got to have a thought process and a culture where the craziest ideas aren't necessarily immediately dismissed because those just might be the best innovations," Bernard insists. "You can't just say 'That's not possible'—it's better to say, 'wait a minute, could that be possible?' "

Having such a culture as well as confidence in his idea was Bernard's initial motivation. However, Sater's PhotoVolt technology was initially dismissed by members of the PV field. Neil explains, "Because our technology is radically different from what's out there, we faced market resistance to change. It's yet another barrier we have to battle through, but if we can penetrate the market, it'll give us a more sustainable position." And Bernard was ready to overcome his disenchantment and to prove the market wrong. "Nobody else would have the commitment to do what had to be done to develop my concept," Bernard says. "It was me or nobody. And I wasn't prepared to watch it die on the vine. I believed so strongly in its potential."

Though Neil feels inspired and motivated by the opportunity to participate in forming the direction of renewable energy, he also feels that American society doesn't foster entrepreneurialism. "There doesn't seem to be a strong voice within our society encouraging people to start a new business themselves. That's a fundamental problem and somehow we need to wake people up and get them to think careers can be more than just a job working for somebody else," he insists. He feels that such an emphasis on the traditional model of "completing school, learning a trade, and working for someone else" is even more pronounced in regions like Northeast Ohio because this is a place where older, more established industries have flourished. He believes the best thing for the Northeast Ohio region is to find a balance between supporting existing industries and encouraging innovation and entrepreneurship in developing industries.

To aspiring innovators, Bernard encourages them to follow their instincts as he did. "Realize that it will be a tough, uphill battle to accomplish what you set out to do. The path won't be easy and you'll have many setbacks along the way," he warns. Bernard says that success requires, "a lot more expertise than what one person will normally have, so you must find people who will be willing to help with your endeavor."

Ways to Overcome Barriers

I had to get people to believe in me and my service. I found a couple of doctors to trust me and I came through for them as I promised. Then they helped me promote my business by word of mouth.
—Ronald Bucci, Administrative Director, MetroHealth (Cleveland)

The largest barrier that Sunflower Solutions had, and in some ways still has, is that our customer base is very untraditional. We sell mostly to nonprofits which plan their budgets up to a year in advance and there is no easy way to find them. The small organization that is doing great work with a clinic in Togo Africa isn't out there advertising themselves, so we have to work hard and go through a lot of channels to find them.
—Christopher Clark, CEO, Sunflower Solutions (Shaker Heights)

Our main competition was Pillsbury, who had a larger sales force, a better distribution network, and a great infrastructure. Our strategy was to develop customized products for larger accounts where they could have proprietary products and differentiation. Pillsbury was less likely to take on this type of business because it was not long-run production type products and could, therefore, cause disruption to their system. Our entire system *was* customization so we could be very efficient at it and be able to compete very favorably against them.
—Steven Marks, Founder, Main Street Gourmet (Cuyahoga Falls)

Financial issues and space issues have been the major challenges over the years. We solved the space issue by expanding very successfully to provide the space the institution and the community needed. Our financial goals remain elusive, in large part due to the two stock market collapses of the past twelve years, which negatively impacted our investments. Additionally, the local environment does not prioritize arts and culture as a key philanthropic concern.
—Mitchell Kahan, Director Emeritus, Akron Art Museum

Ways to Overcome Barriers (cont'd.)

Early on, I was considered an outsider to the existing photovoltaic community, which made it difficult to find support for my invention. Nevertheless, I realized this experience was a common problem with new technologies because many major breakthroughs originate outside the established industry and are initially rejected by insiders. I overcame this by staying focused and continuing to fight to demonstrate the commercial viability of my invention.
—Bernard Sater, Cofounder, GreenField Solar (Oberlin)

We had both technical and business barriers. We are still overcoming them as we go since the terrain constantly changes. We accomplished our goals by bringing the right talent and being nimble. In particular, we recognized that we needed to constantly change if we are to succeed.
—Bahman Taheri, CEO, AlphaMicron, Inc. (Kent)

With our high service approach to caring for customers, we required higher profit margins. To achieve them required quality staffing and training programs to enhance performance and efficiency issues. We developed our profit centers, expanded them, and dominated rather than shared the market with our competitors.
—Russ Vernon, Retired Chairman, West Point Market (Akron)

In science and technology, I continuously have to overcome gender bias. Unfortunately, it is an ongoing process and I am always trying new methods. It's extremely hard work.
—Judit E. Puskas, Professor, The University of Akron

In order to enter the biomedical space, capital was needed. I was viewed solely as a novice businessman with no credibility by investors. The confidence was slowly earned by success in the market.
—David Kay, Cofounder, OrthoHelix Surgical Designs (Medina)

Ways to Overcome Barriers (cont'd.)

Our largest barrier was offering a new service that was not recognized by a new brand that businesses were not familiar with. To overcome this, we had to show a track record of success so we made a few case studies from clients that we had been working with. We decided that the best way to market this was to speak in front of large audiences that had an interest in expanding their businesses so we partnered with several local chambers and offered to present on driving business with social media.

—Shon Christy, Founder, Christy Creative (Akron)

Part III
Educating Future Innovators

Progress Is the Product

Thomas V. Chema

Although it might be trendy today to have a "life plan," I am proud to be one of those folks who stepped off the career track once or twice and took that road less traveled. I didn't grow up hoping to be an entrepreneur—or a college president for that matter. In fact, I was the first in my family to even go to college. Unlike today's students, I didn't conduct a nationwide search or tour any campuses looking for just the right school. The Notre Dame nuns who taught me at St. Aloysius in East Liverpool, Ohio, said the University of Notre Dame was the only place to go and that's where I went.

People encouraged me to go to law school, and after graduating from Harvard, I joined a large firm in Cleveland. Entrepreneurship wasn't even discussed in those days and taking a career risk was frowned upon. I can still remember how disappointed my hard-working, steelworker father was when I announced I was leaving a lucrative law practice for a public service position paying $46,000 a year. After heading the Ohio Lottery, I served as chair of the Public Utilities Commission. Handling those management and business challenges while working for the government was great preparation for my next job.

In 1989, Governor Dick Celeste called and asked me to help put together a public/private partnership to build a baseball and basketball complex in downtown Cleveland. Taking that big idea and turning it into the reality of Jacobs Field and Gund Arena was definitely an entrepreneurial move—even if I didn't realize it at the time. What we were engaged in during the five-year process was really the height of entrepreneurship. Looking back, we also helped a couple of businesses get started and pushed lots of entrepreneurial activity into what is now known as the Historic Gateway District on East Fourth Street in downtown Cleveland. In fact, our support even helped Hard Hatted Women get a foothold in the construction industry in Northeast Ohio.

By the time the Gateway complex was up and running, I had really embraced the concept of entrepreneurship. My passion—then and now—focused on bringing people together with new ideas and projects. Once again, I reinvented my career. This time, I launched my own consulting business to create similar sports and entertainment developments in other cities.

In the early 1990s, I also joined the Board of Trustees at Hiram College. As a board member for eleven years, I made the scenic thirty-five-mile trip from Cleveland for quarterly meetings. I wanted to be a board member for a number of reasons. Making the connection to such a quality liberal arts college was a way for me to further the cause of education, which has always been important to me. I believe that the higher education system is a vehicle for reaching the ideals first proposed by the ancient Greeks. To be candid, I knew that being a member of the board of trustees of a college would enhance my personal prestige. My other motive was to get to know people I wanted to know who served on the board.

What I didn't see coming was accepting the job of president of Hiram College. Ten years ago when Hiram faced serious financial trouble and a vacancy in the President's Office, members of the board of trustees didn't sift through stacks of vitas and reference letters from academics across the country. They turned across the table and asked me—a fellow trustee—to take the job. I was flattered, of course, and surprised. Almost immediately, I began to make the connections and could see that my nontraditional path as an attorney, public servant, business developer, and now entrepreneur had uniquely prepared me for the challenge.

What is interesting now is seeing just how much I used my entrepreneurial skills in my new position. Once I was president, it was clear that Hiram College needed to embrace a new way of doing things and that included examining our financial situation with an entrepreneurial mind-set. Like almost all colleges and universities, Hiram struggled financially. Our enrollment was declining, but our cost structure was going in the opposite direction. Today, we have successfully balanced our budget and have begun to whittle away at the accumulated deficit resulting from "the sins of the past." In order to be both financially and academically viable, we needed a student body approaching twelve hundred, not seven hundred. We've met that goal.

Exploring and creating additional revenue streams has been a priority. Hiram Ventures, Inc., our newly-developed business arm, was formed as a for-profit subsidiary to allow the college to benefit from revenue generated from its ideas and activities. Linking entrepreneurial ideas from faculty and students with Hiram Ventures has proven to be a great fit. One example is the Hiram Genomics Store, the first of what we hope will be a number of partnerships on campus, that will help generate funds for the college. An educator-to-educator enterprise based on nine years of outreach experience, the Hiram Genomics Store offers DNA-based technology and products for use by high school and community college teachers. Started in 2010 by a biology professor and four of his students, the first line of products involves a classroom test kit involving DNA analysis, providing reagents and services for DNA isolation, PCR, and gel electrophoresis.

Along with this initiative, five years ago the college received substantial grants from the Ewing Marion Kauffman Foundation's Kauffman Campuses Initiative and Burton D. Morgan Foundation's Northeast Ohio Collegiate Entrepreneurship Program. This support allowed our faculty members to begin incorporating entrepreneurship into their courses—an important first step in encouraging students to consider entrepreneurship as a career path. On our campus another popular idea is called Student Run Ventures, where students and faculty join in starting businesses, such as an artisan bakery run by first-year students and a French professor. Our experience shows that students are impacted not only by changes in curriculum, but also by the attitudes and outlook of their professors toward the world of business. Thanks to the entrepreneurship model, our faculty members, administrators, and students are much more open and receptive to new ways of thinking and different approaches to solving problems. In 2010, the college officially named Integrated Entrepreneurship a Center of Distinction. Hiram's seven Centers of Distinction combine the power of Hiram's core arts and sciences with rich interdisciplinary programs in ethics, business, biotechnology, leadership, environment, writing, medical humanities, and entrepreneurship. The centers provide abundant experiences for Hiram's students, expand the college's reach to the broader community, and reflect its mission.

Perhaps our most far-reaching, entrepreneurial idea is to build a retirement village on campus. Although we've hit some roadblocks, the project is now on track and will include individual homes, townhouses, and eventually an assisted living center. The college will provide "sizzle" to this endeavor by allowing—and encouraging—residents to take classes, attend lectures, concerts, art exhibits, and athletic events. Residents would be able to use our library and fitness center. We hope that they will want to mentor our students and otherwise contribute to the life of the college, while enhancing their own academic fitness.

I have always believed in the power of a liberal arts education and my tenure at Hiram College has only solidified those feelings. Today, however, I am focused on making sure that leaders in Northeast Ohio understand that innovation and entrepreneurship is not just the province of our large state universities. I'm encouraging business people and politicians also to look to liberal arts colleges such as John Carroll, Baldwin Wallace, and Hiram for new ideas. Innovation is not only about expensive, cutting-edge technologies, but rather comes from individuals who approach challenges and understand issues in a new way. In order to better support innovation and entrepreneurship in Northeast Ohio, we ought to be supporting the kind of spirit and culture which is the basis of a liberal arts education.

As I look back on my career, I find it interesting that my tenure as president of Hiram College is the longest I've stayed at any job. For a guy who likes to throw lots of ideas at the wall and see what sticks, this has turned out to be a place where I wanted to stick around. I believe two of my personality traits really helped me succeed as a president—and as an entrepreneur. I don't give up easily, and I am not afraid of uncertainty. However, my lack of patience can be a problem and sometimes has made things more difficult. I can't emphasize enough that people must not be afraid of uncertainty. Far too many people consider "risk" a four-letter word. These folks are negative and only think about all the bad things that can happen. Risk really is all about how much one is willing to gamble that the uncertainty can be made to turn out positively. We live in an inherently chaotic world, and history shows that we are always looking for certainty and order. But to succeed and advance as individuals and as a society we need new ideas—or at the minimum—repackaged ideas. The best entrepreneurs draw from both their experiences and the lessons learned from others. Then they take the risk. Progress is the product.

Note: This article was written prior to Chema's retirement from Hiram.

Words of Advice

Be careful, but not too careful. Be focused, but be aware of everything. Be ready to fail horribly by others' definition. Be peaceful in the storm. And be aware that you can't do this by yourself—always appreciate the work of your team.

—David Kay, Cofounder, OrthoHelix Surgical Designs (Medina)

First, obtain the best education available to you. Have a curious and creative mind, seek unmet needs, and find gaps in the marketplace. Look for opportunities where your skills and passions can challenge you and drive your success. Starting a new business is not for "sissies" and free enterprise is not free. It is unforgiving.

—Russ Vernon, Retired Chairman, West Point Market (Akron)

When you feel the most risk, you are the closest. Push through your fear and worry and get to the other side. Most people give up when they are confronted with fear, but the true innovators are the ones that have the courage to get through.

—Shon Christy, Founder, Christy Creative (Akron)

Steel yourself against failure. Get used to hearing "no" 99 times for every "yes." Don't be discouraged by those who cannot seem to understand your vision. Be passionate and articulate. Surround yourself with the best people you can find—and get them to drink your Kool-Aid.

—Andrew Vaeth, Founder, Cureo (Wooster)

You will hit road bumps and obstacles along the way that will test your motivation and commitment and will make you question whether or not your idea can actually work. If you don't start the process knowing that you're going to see it through no matter what, you'll stumble around and go through a lot more emotional stress than you need to.

—Christopher Clark, CEO, Sunflower Solutions (Shaker Heights)

Words of Advice (cont'd.)

Build a team. Nobody can do it themselves and nobody has all of the skills necessary to build a successful company. Don't be afraid to give up some of the responsibilities.

—Lauren Wolf, CEO, AeroClay, Inc. (Cleveland)

The only way to have a successful business is to have a product or service that people like enough to pay for and eventually (hopefully sooner rather than later) you can bring in more money than you spend. It doesn't matter what investors think, what economic development professionals think, what the media thinks—if the customers don't like it and don't want to pay for it, you'll be out of business.

—Mike Burkons, Founder, Charitee Golf LLC (Shaker Heights)

Don't spend your time working on something that doesn't excite you personally.

—Michael Mariola, Owner, Sustainable Foods, Inc. (Wooster)

Make sure your invention does not defy the laws of physics. Make sure there is a market for what you plan to invent—just because a gadget you invent works does not mean you can sell it. Do not give up when you fail. If you are stuck in your design, try to see how nature might have solved the same type of problem.

—Majid Rashidi, Professor, Cleveland State University

Trust your instincts and stay focused on what you want to accomplish. Realize that it will be a tough, uphill battle to accomplish what you set out to do. The path won't be easy and you'll have many setbacks along the way. Success will require a lot more expertise than what one person will normally have, but you must find people who will be willing to help with your endeavor."

—Bernard Sater, Cofounder, GreenField Solar (Oberlin)

An Easy Solution to a Modern Problem

Shon Christy

It was his education that enabled Shon Christy to become an innovator and entrepreneur. He attended The University of Akron, majoring in marketing and participating in student groups such as Sigma Nu Fraternity and the International Business Association. These experiences taught Christy the value of networking and provided insight into creating and maintaining relationships with friends, clients, strategic partners, and colleagues. In 2007, Christy began his master's degree work. During his two years of study, he began to notice a change in the ways people were communicating with each other. "As I started embracing social media, I understood that there was a real opportunity to move away from a traditional marketing platform to a social media-based approach," Christy admits.

He defines social media as a true form of permission marketing because the consumers decide what messages he or she is interested in hearing about. He points out, "Technology has advanced so we do not have to listen to the radio ads, because we have satellite radio now, and we don't have to watch commercials on TV, because we have DVR. Therefore, social media outlets become a great outlet for conversations, feedback, and problem solving between consumers, potential consumers, and the company." Christy's awareness of the potential of social media enabled him to quickly solidify Christy Creative as one of the top e-marketing companies in the area. His company enables small business owners to utilize an effective form of advertising that is significantly less expensive than traditional advertising. "Today, you cannot see an advertisement that doesn't include *Like Us on Facebook* or *Follow Us on Twitter*. The small business owner knows that they need to be involved in social media marketing, but it is a challenge because most of them play the role of CEO, CFO, HR, marketing, and customer service on a daily basis—leaving little time for adding new ideas and processes." It's easy to see why small business owners accepted Christy and his team with open arms: Christy Creative, was offering them an easy solution to a modern problem.

Founded in 2010, Christy Creative revised and refined their business strategy multiple times. Though there were companies already offering social media programs for companies and consulting, Christy realized there were no companies that offered management of these medias for small business owners. "What we found was that small business owners were too busy to actively manage campaigns even if they understood social media, so we focused on building a program that focused on solving one of the key issues: time. Shifting our focus has set our company apart from the rest of our competition," Christy explains. His company helps local, small business owners gain a competitive edge and, ultimately, level the playing field in the marketing arena. Shon Christy sees small businesses as critical to the success of local communities. He believes, "It is very rewarding to be a part of their success."

Christy Creative enables small businesses to utilize top social media websites like Facebook, Twitter, YouTube, LinkedIn, Google+, Yelp, and Foursquare to get consumer attention. Creating a relationship-oriented presence on these websites allows Christy Creative to help small businesses listen to their customers, and to help answer their questions. Christy also helps small business owners analyze customers' responses to their media, such as liking them on Facebook or following them on Twitter, so owners know exactly what their consumers want.

The media marketing business has proven to be challenging in ways Christy did not expect: "I knew that social media was changing the marketing world, what I did not anticipate was the speed that social media would change." Over the past two years, the company has had to add outlets for Google+ and Pinterest as well as adapt to drastic changes in the Facebook platform (this year, Facebook implemented its new "timeline" format). All of Christy Creative customers had to be transitioned over to the new format in a very short period of time. Christy finds that social media is about consistency and focuses on holding valuable conversations through this media. Such focus has allowed him to become a talented problem solver for both his clients and their customers.

However, there were some problems in the beginning. "Our largest barrier was offering a new service that was not recognized as a new brand that businesses were familiar with." But Christy Creative didn't let that stop them. They were quick to prove their successful strategy and track record by presenting new clients with case studies which illustrated their work. The company also chose to market themselves to large audiences; they partnered with several local chambers and offered to do presentations on driving business with social media to groups of businesses who were interested in expanding. It wasn't long before their client list began to grow. Since then, Christy has cofounded two new companies, eat.drink.promote (a national niche e-marketing firm, focused on the restaurant and bar industry) and luxuryhomelocator.com (a high-end real estate search site).

Shon Christy believes risk taking has contributed exciting things to his company. It inspires him to be more motivated and innovative. "Entrepreneurs just look at risk differently. Jimmy Carter once said, 'Go out on a limb. That's where the fruit is.' I believe that to grow, we need to climb the tree and go out on those branches where others are not comfortable to create a positive change and innovation in our respective fields," he insists. He challenges his team to go out on to those branches through brainstorming sessions. He finds that the company's best ideas come from these sessions because someone always plays the devil's advocate. This technique allows many people to contribute to the conversation and produce diverse ideas. "Our first rule is always: there is no such thing as a stupid idea. Many times our final solutions are a combination of ideas generated through our strategic brainstorming sessions," Christy explains.

Ultimately, Christy feels his success at Christy Creative is rooted in his family. It was through loans from his immediate family that he was able to support the venture from its inception. Furthermore, he credits his business skills to the values his family taught him as a child. He was inspired by his grandfathers, who both served in the armed forces, and by his parents, who showed him that hard work truly pays off. But, most importantly, family serves as Christy's primary motivation for all that he achieves—not only in the marketing arena, but in his personal life as well. Recently, Christy was elected vice president of the Board of Directors for the Up Side of Downs, a community-oriented organization which works with individuals who have been diagnosed with Down Syndrome and their families. Christy became involved with the organization in 2010, shortly after he and his wife found out their son would be born with Downs. He is also involved in the Akron Rotary Club, another community-oriented organization dedicated to service above self.

Christy believes Northeast Ohio can do much more to support innovation and entrepreneurship in the region. He suggests, as a first step, bringing more technology, entrepreneurial, and emerging media-based conferences to the area. "I think that once people get a true feel for the area and the opportunities that exist here, they become inspired to move forward," Christy believes. But, these innovators cannot succeed unless Northeast Ohio provides them with a support network. Having outlets that would specifically support innovators and entrepreneurs outside of local incubators and accelerators is essential to success in the region.

He also believes that in order to create entrepreneurs, education and discussion should start at a young age. It should be available to young individuals at all levels of education, not just in the world of higher education. Christy insists entrepreneurship deserves to be a high priority in education. To aspiring innovators, he advises, "When you feel the most risk, you are the closest. Push through your fear and worry and get to the other side. Most people give up when they are confronted with fear, but the true innovators are the ones that have the courage to get through."

Ways Education Influences Entrepreneurship

My education included a lot of communication and philosophy which, when combined with technical courses, makes it easy for me to communicate with investors, customers, and our company.
—John Lauletta, CEO/CTO, Exacter, Inc. (Columbus)

Every step of my education, from middle school to the end of my PhD program, has played a significant role in my work as a designer and inventor.
—Majid Rashidi, Professor, Cleveland State University

I have been a lifetime student of business. I developed a library of business books, attended industry seminars, took night school classes, and gained experience working in the business.
—Russ Vernon, Retired Chairman, West Point Market (Akron)

My accounting background and experience at a large CPA firm was instrumental. I learned many systems and concepts that I was able to employ, such as expense reports, basic accounting, cost accounting, invoicing, and segregation of duties.
—Steven Marks, Founder, Main Street Gourmet (Cuyahoga Falls)

Though I studied business and even had a focus in entrepreneurship, the biggest education process came from my own experiences in the field and from my own board of advisors. Formal education can only lay the foundation for entrepreneurship—which is critical—but since every venture is different, it ultimately is up to the entrepreneur.
—Christopher Clark, CEO, Sunflower Solutions (Shaker Heights)

My education in polymer science and biochemistry played a decisive part in my invention, but not in my venture.
—Joseph Kennedy, Professor, The University of Akron

Ways Education Influences Entrepreneurship (cont'd.)

My education played an instrumental role in how I decided to approach my venture. I have an amazing marketing education from The University of Akron that is the base of all of my business knowledge. Equally as important is the understanding of relationships and networking that I received early in my collegiate career through student groups such as Sigma Nu Fraternity and the International Business Association. All of these groups introduced me to friends, clients, strategic partners, and colleagues across the country who have assisted me along the way.

—Shon Christy, Founder, Christy Creative (Akron)

I was educated in Hungary in a completely different system. Nothing was handed to us—we had to improvise. At the same time, it was an excellent system that gave me a well-rounded education.

—Judit E. Puskas, Professor, The University of Akron

My scientific education has been extremely helpful in training me to be exact and to be able to look at things both broadly and in fine detail. The experience I have had to teach has provided me the opportunity to learn how to communicate concepts and how to motivate others. My true business education, however, has come through key mentors and the actual experience of building a company.

—Hiroyuki Fujita, President & CEO, Quality Electrodynamics (Mayfield Village)

Appendix

Companies that Lend Helping Hands

The following organizations are dedicated to supporting and promoting entrepreneurial ventures in the Northeast Ohio region. Some are involved more directly with regional businesses while others are effective from a distance, (for example, some are involved in local and national politics on behalf of regional business ventures). Please note that this is not a list of organizations which simply provide funding for entrepreneurial ventures, though such opportunities are offered by some of the organizations on this list. For more information, please visit their websites.

BioEnterprise

www.bioenterprise.com

BioEnterprise is an initiative which is designed specifically to aid the growth of health care companies and to commercialize bioscience technologies. It is partnered with the Cleveland Clinic, University Hospitals, Case Western Reserve University, Summa Health System, and BioInnovation Institute in Akron as well as other technology partners. Each year, the organization selects a number of companies to help them achieve greater levels of success. These companies are typically selected because of their research regarding biotechnology, an innovative medical device, or their focus on health care services.

BioEnterprise's strategy includes bioscience management guidance, cultivating relationships with world-class research and clinical institutions, increased access to capital, development through the support of strategic partnerships, and a reliance on their network of regional business capabilities.

Cleveland Plus, Team NEO

www.clevelandplusbusiness.com

Cleveland Plus is a regional marketing campaign. The campaign, managed by Regional Marketing Alliance, is directed towards entrepreneurs looking for a place to start their business. By marketing the region, Cleveland Plus hopes to attract businesses and talent to Northeast Ohio. They describe the region as affordable, offer access to other Cleveland Plus companies (which allows key business and community leaders to communicate), and emphasize the importance of manufacturing to the region's heritage. Cleveland Plus' website offers access to important information for entrepreneurs, including access to demographics and workforce, quarterly economic reports, Ohio tax reform, incentives and tax credits, higher education, and more.

Team NEO exists within the Cleveland Plus organization and was founded by FirstEnergy Corporation, the Greater Akron Chamber, the Stark Development Board, the Lorain County Chamber of Commerce, the Youngstown-Warren Regional Chamber, and the Greater Cleveland Partnership. The goal of Team NEO is to align the region's economic development efforts, to market the region, to attract new business, and to increase collaboration among the region's key economic development groups to support growth and job creation.

Council of Smaller Enterprises (COSE)

www.cose.org

This is the largest small business support organization in the region. COSE offers cost-effective group purchasing programs, networking, and educational resources to Northeast Ohio small businesses.

Though their primary objective is to increase small business growth, the company also advocates for the interests and priorities of smaller enterprises. The organization has a long history of fighting for the rights of all small business owners in local and federal policy.

Fund for Our Economic Future

www.futurefundneo.org

The Fund for Our Economic Future describes themselves as "a collaboration of philanthropic organizations and individuals that have united to strengthen the economic competitiveness of Northeast Ohio through grant-making, research and civic engagement." The organization aims to increase regional competitiveness through a stimulation of business growth, talent development, racial and economic inclusion, and government collaboration. Their long-term goal is to revitalize the region. The Fund is partnered with many of the other organizations on this list, including BioEnterprise, JumpStart, MAGNET, NorTech, Team NEO, and Towards Employment.

Greater Cleveland Partnership

www.gcpartnership.com

Created in March 2004, the Greater Cleveland Partnership now boasts more than fifteen thousand members as well as a small-business partner, the Council of Smaller Enterprises (COSE). It is a membership association limited to Northeast Ohio companies and organizations and is also one of the largest metropolitan chambers of commerce in the United States. The organization is dedicated to mobilizing private sector leadership, expanding the availability of expertise and resources in the region, creating jobs, growing investments, and improving the economic conditions of Northeast Ohio.

JumpStart

www.jumpstartinc.org

JumpStart was created in 2003 after a regional group, made up of civic, community, and philanthropic leaders, came together to discuss how to repair the region and restore jobs and wealth to the greater Cleveland area. The organization invests directly in high growth entrepreneurial companies in the area. JumpStart also works to raise funds for other support organizations and it manages a network of twenty incubators, accelerators, and investors. The company's main goal is to increase the economic impact and sustainability of, what they call, Northeast Ohio's "entrepreneurial ecosystem" (which they define as "the interconnected and diverse organizations that support entrepreneurial companies").

Manufacturing Advocacy and Growth Network (MAGNET)

www.manufacturingsuccess.org
This nonprofit organization was founded in 1984 and has since been dedicated to supporting and educating manufacturers, in an attempt to improve their competitiveness and growth. The ultimate goal of MAGNET is to transform Ohio's economy into a powerful, global player. The organization utilizes a board of directors, which provides leadership for the manufacturers, which includes representatives from local companies, universities, and economic development organizations. The organization also provides consulting services, process improvement programs, and increased productivity programs. MAGNET is one of the Edison Technology Centers, as designated by the state of Ohio, and is a provider of Manufacturing Extension Partnership (MEP) services, as funded by the National Institute of Standards and Technology.

NorTech

www.nortech.org

NorTech describes itself as "a regional nonprofit technology-based economic development organization serving twenty-one counties in Northeast Ohio." The organization leads efforts to develop regional innovation clusters in an attempt to create jobs, attract capital, and encourage a long-term, positive economic impact. NorTech works intimately with businesses to build relationships among their cluster members and to find funding, research, and business opportunities. The organization is also involved in a broader sense, serving as a liaison to federal and state government and policy leaders, working to develop strategies that enhance cluster growth. NorTech is currently focused on two specific industries: advanced energy and flexible electronics.

PolymerOhio, Inc.

www.polymerohio.org

An Ohio Edison Technology Center, PolymerOhio focuses on enhancing polymer industry throughout the state. The organization helps polymer companies establish global competitiveness and sustain growth. PolymerOhio employees are experts in the field of polymer technology; knowledgeable in the materials, processes, and products. Though the organization is supported by member dues (as well as the Ohio Department of Development), PolymerOhio provides members with a wealth of resources, including: access to academic institutions, economic development resources, and service providers that enable continual growth and improvement.

TechSolve

www.techsolve.org

TechSolve was founded in 1982 by the city of Cincinnati, the Greater Cincinnati Chamber of Commerce, the University of Cincinnati, and corporations throughout the region. The objective was to create an organization which could assist local manufacturing suppliers to improve efficiency and competitiveness in a global market. Focusing on small to midsized companies, TechSolve helps identify and prioritize the best improvement opportunities for companies in a wide range of industries. In 2005, the organization began consulting businesses in the health care industry. Most noteworthy is TechSolve's emphasis on collaboration and their focus on teaching small businesses how to implement the improvement tools and processes themselves, rather than having an outside company control them.

Towards Employment (WorkAdvance)

www.towardsemployment.org

Since 1976, Towards Employment has been dedicated to enabling "individuals to achieve and maintain self-sufficiency through employment" in the Greater Cleveland area. The organization's mission is to prepare disadvantaged adults to find jobs, keep these jobs, and continually move up the career ladder. Starting in 2004, the organization also began to place exoffenders in permanent full-time jobs. Towards Employment uses a holistic approach based on research which has proven that combining job-readiness training, supportive services, and access to vocational training enables people coming off of welfare, out of prison, or from the streets to succeed in the job market. The organization collaborates with other agencies (ranging from other job-seeking agencies, to recovery resources, to education resources) as well as with Cleveland-area employers. Towards Employment focuses on tailoring their programs to the needs of the employers they support. The organization also offers support services and coaching to entry-level workers to improve retention rates for their partnered employees.

WIRE-Net

www.wire-net.org

WIRE-Net was founded in 1988 in an attempt to help manufacturing jobs stay in the Cleveland area. Today, the organization continues to serve manufacturers and is a catalyst for economic growth in the region. WIRE-Net provides manufacturing firms with core strategies to remain resilient and to ensure long-term profitability; it is the only organization in the region working exclusively with manufacturers. WIRE-Net focuses on not only improving production, but also on human resource management, training and education, and expansion opportunities. They also serve as an advocate for manufacturing firms in regards to new investments, real estate opportunities, and government issues. WIRE-Net works to connect leaders throughout the region to one another and to engage these leaders in their communities. By strengthening these businesses, WIRE-Net fosters healthy communities and fuels economic growth.

Entrepreneurship and Business Programs in Northeast Ohio

Ashland University*

Offers: Business Administration (BA); Business Management (BSBA); Entrepreneurship (BSBA); International Business (BSBA)
Website: www.ashland.edu/departments/business-management

Baldwin Wallace College

Offers: (Undergraduate) Business Administration; Accounting; Finance; Healthcare Management; Human Resource Management; Innovation and Entrepreneurship; International Business; Management; and Marketing. (MBA) Management; Accounting; Entrepreneurship; Executive Management; Healthcare Management; Human Resources; International Management; and Sustainability
Website: www.bw.edu/academics/bus/ug

Bowling Green State University

Offers: Accounting; Economics; Business; Business Education; Finance; Management; Marketing; and Marketing Education
Website: www.business.bgsu.edu
Case Western Reserve University
Offers: (Undergraduate) Majors: Accounting (BS); Management (BS); Economics (BA). Minors: Accounting, Business Management,

Finance, Economics, Entrepreneurship, Marketing. (MBA) Executive, Global, Accounting, Finance (MSM), Operations Research / Supply Chain (MSM), Positive Organization Development (MS). (Doctorate): Management, Organizational Behavior, Operations Research.
Website: weatherhead.case.edu

Chancellor University

Offers: (Undergraduate) Accounting; Marketing; Management; Finance; Management Information Systems. (MBA) Business Administration; (MA) Management
Website: www.chancelloru.edu/college-of-business.aspx

Cleveland State University

Offers: (Undergraduate) Majors: Accounting, Business Administration, Business Economics, Finance, Information Systems and Technology, International Business, Management & Labor Relations, Marketing, Operations & Supply Chain Management. Minors: Accounting, Business, Computer & Information Science, Information Systems, International Business, Finance, Management & Labor Relations, Marketing, Operations & Supply Chain Management. (MBA) Accounting, Economic Development, Finance, Healthcare Administration, Human Resources & Labor Relations, Information Systems, International Business, Marketing, Operations & Supply Chain Management.
Website: www.csuohio.edu/business

The College of Wooster*

Offers: Economics; Business Economics
Website: www.wooster.edu/academics/areas/economics

Cuyahoga County Community College

Offers: Accounting; Business Management; Human Resource Management; Industrial Distribution; International Business; Public Administration; Small Business Management; Economics; Lodging-Tourism Management; Restaurant/Food Service Management;

Business Solutions (Information Technology); Marketing; Office Operations Management; Purchasing and Supply Management
Website: www.tri-c.edu/programs/businessmanagement/business
(Note: this is a two-year community and technical college)

Heidelberg University

Offers: (Undergraduate) Accounting; Business Administration; Economics; (MBA) Business Administration
Website: www.heidelberg.edu/academiclife/depts/business

Hiram College*

Offers: Accounting and Financial Management; Management; Economics; Entrepreneurship (minor)
Website: www.hiram.edu/economics

John Carroll University

Offers: (Undergraduate) Accounting; Economics; Finance; Human Resources; International Business with Language and Culture; Logistics; Management; Marketing; Entrepreneurship (minor). (MBA) Integrated Business Decision; (MS) Accountancy; 5th Year MBA Program
Website: www.jcu.edu/boler

Kent State University

Offers: (Undergraduate) Accounting; Economics; Finance; Management and Information Systems; Marketing and Entrepreneurship. (MS) Financial Engineering; (MAE) Economics; Financial Economics; (MSA) Accounting; Assurance Services; Taxation; (MBA) Accounting; Business Administration; Economics; Fashion Design and Merchandising; Finance; Human Resource Management; Information Systems; Marketing; Supply Chain Management; Business Administration-Professional. (PhD) Accounting; Finance; Human Resource Management; International Economics; Marketing; Operations Management; Strategic Management.
Website: www.kent.edu/business

Denison University*

Offers: Philosophy, Politics, and Economics; Economics
Website: denison.edu/academics/economics

Lake Erie College

Offers: (Undergraduate) Accounting; Forensic Accounting; Advertising, Public Relations, and Digital Media; Arts Management; Business Administration; Entrepreneurship; Equine Entrepreneurship; Finance; Human Resource Management; International Business; Management; Marketing; Sport Management. (MBA) Business Administration
Website: www.lec.edu/programs/business.php

Malone University

Offers: (Undergraduate) Accounting; Business Administration; Business Information Systems (Computer Science); Economics (minor); Finance (minor); Management (minor); Marketing Management; Marketing (minor); Organizational Management; Project Management; Public Relations (Communication Arts); Sport Management. (MBA) Business Administration; (MA) Organizational Leadership
Website: www.malone.edu/academics/sbl

Muskingum University

Offers: Accounting; Business; International Business; Economics
Website: www.muskingum.edu/dept/eab

Notre Dame College

Offers: Accounting; Business Administration; Human Resources Development; International Business, Management; Marketing; Sport Management; Public Relations; Entrepreneurship (minor); Financial Services Management (minor)
Website: www.notredamecollege.edu/academics/academic-divisions/business-administration

Oberlin College

Offers: Economics; Business; Entrepreneurship (classes offered through the Creativity and Leadership Project)
Website: www.oberlin.edu/arts-and-sciences/departments/economics

OSU Agricultural Technology Institute

Offers: Business Management; Construction Management; Crop Management and Soil Conservation; Dairy Cattle Production and Management; Floral Design and Marketing; Greenhouse and Nursery Management; Agricultural Business; Agricultural Systems Management; Food Business Management
Website: www.ati.osu.edu

Tiffin University

Offers: (Undergraduate) Accounting; Computer and Information Technology; Finance; Global Leadership Honors; Management; Equine Business; Hospitality and Tourism; Human Resources Management; International Business; Managerial Studies; Marketing; Sports and Recreation Management; Sports and Athletic Administration; Recreation and Tourism; Sports Marketing. (MBA) Business Administration; Finance; General Management; Healthcare Administration; Human Resource Management; International Business; Leadership; Marketing; Sport Management
Website: www.tiffin.edu/business

The University of Akron

Offers: (Undergraduate) Accounting; Finance; General Business; Human Resource Management; Information Systems Management; Integrated Marketing Communications; International Business; Marketing Management; Sales Management; Supply Chain/Operations Management; Consumer Marketing (minor); Database Marketing (minor); Direct Interactive Marketing (minor); Entrepreneurship (minor); Financial Planning (minor); Management Information Systems (minor). (MBA): Leadership and Organizational Change,

Interdisciplinary, Finance, Direct Interactive Marketing, International Business, International Finance, Global Technology Innovation, Health Care Management, Supply Chain Management, Strategic Marketing, Management
Website: www.uakron.edu/cba

University of Mount Union

Offers: Accounting; Financial Mathematics; Healthcare Management; Human Resource Management; Marketing; Financial Planning; International Business and Economics; Public Relations; Finance; Management; Sport Business; Business Administration (minor); Entrepreneurship (minor)
Website: www.mountunion.edu/undergraduate-programs

Ursuline College

Offers: (Undergraduate) Accounting; Business Administration; Management Information Systems; Public Relations and Marketing Communications; Sport Management. (MBA) Business
Website: www.ursuline.edu/Academics/Graduate_Professional

Walsh University

Offers: Accounting; Global Business; Management; Marketing
Website: www.walsh.edu/deville-school-of-business

Youngstown State University

Offers: (Undergraduate) Accounting; Business Economics; Business Administration; Business Technology; Merchandising: Fashion and Interiors; Finance; Management; Human Resource Management; Management Information Systems; Marketing Management; Advertising and Public Relations. (MBA) Business Administration; (MA) Economics; Financial Economics
Website: web.ysu.edu/wcba

*=*Schools with Burton D. Morgan Centers for Entrepreneurship*

Note: This is not a comprehensive list.

Notes

1. Diane Suchetka, "After years of hurdles, Cleveland's medical mart officially opens with an Oct. 8 ribbon-cutting," *Cleveland.com*, Oct. 02, 2013, http://www.cleveland.com/business/index.ssf/2013/10/after_years_of_hurdles_clevela.html.

2. W. Dennis Keating and Thomas Bier, "Greater Cleveland's First Suburbs Consortium: Fighting Sprawl and Urban Decline," *Housing Policy Debate* 19, no. 3 (2007).

3. Richey Piiparien, "Not Dead Yet: The Infill of Cleveland's Urban Core," *MetroTrends Urban Institute*, 2012, http://www.metrotrends.org/spotlight/Cleveland_Spotlight.cfm.

4. Richey Piiparien and Jim Russell, "Globalizing Cleveland: A Path Forward," *EngagedScholarship@CSU*, last modified May 1, 2014, http://engagedscholarship.csuohio.edu/urban_facpub/1164.

5. Harlan Spector, "Improvements to Urban Roadways Called Crucial to Economic Growth, *The Plain Dealer* (Cleveland, OH), July 20, 2012.

6. Daniel Denvir, "The 10 Most Segregated Urban Areas in America," *Salon Media Group, Inc.*, March 29, 2011, http://www.salon.com/2011/03/29/most_segregated_cities/.

7. Claudia J. Coulton and Julian Chow, "The Impact of Poverty on Cleveland's Neighborhoods," in *Cleveland: A Metropolitan Reader*, ed. W. Dennis Keating, Norman Krumholz, and David C. Perry (Kent: Kent State University Press, 1995).

8. "Welcome to NEO CANDO," *Case Western Reserve University*, July 18, 2014, http://neocando.case.edu/.

9. "Section 8 Demographic Report" (Internal report, Cuyahoga Metropolitan Housing Authority, 2012), 1.

10. Alex Kotlowitz, "All Boarded Up," *The New York Times* (New York, NY), Mar. 4, 2009.

11. Keating, W. Dennis, *Cuyahoga County Land Reutilization Corporation the Beginning, the Present, and Beyond*, Cuyahoga: Cuyahoga Land Bank, 2011, http://www.cuyahogalandbank.org/articles/CCLRC_2009_2011_Report.pdf.

12. *Re-Imagining a More Sustainable Cleveland.* Kent: Kent State University Cleveland Urban Design Collaborative, 2011. http://www.scribd.com/doc/64257913/Re-Imagining-A-More-Sustainable-Cleveland-Report.

13. "US2010," *Brown University*, July 18, 2014, http://www.s4.brown.edu/us2010/index.htm.

14. *The New American City Faces its Regional Future.*

15. John A. Hostetler, *Amish Society* (Baltimore: Johns-Hopkins University Press, 1980).

16. "Milestones: 1974," *U.S. Equal Employment Opportunity Commission*, August 8, 2014. http://www.eeoc.gov/eeoc/history/35th/milestones/1974.html.

17. Irving Janis, *Groupthink: Psychological Studies of Policy Decisions and Fiascoes* (New York: Houghton Mifflin, 1982).

18. Irving Janis, *Groupthink: Psychological Studies of Policy Decisions and Fiascoes* (New York: Houghton Mifflin, 1982), 9.

19. "The 2014 NAFE Top 50 Companies for Executive Women," *Working Mother*, August 8, 2014. http://www.workingmother.com/best-company-list/151009.

20. "AT&T Women Leaders," *AT&T*, August 8, 2014. http://www.att.com/gen/general?pid=23873.

21. David Neumark, Brandon Wall, and Junfu Zhang, "Do Small Businesses Create More Jobs? New Evidence from the National Establishment Time Series," *The Review of Economics and Statistics* 93, no. 1 (2011): 16–29.

22. "Innovation in American Regions," *Indiana Business Research Center*, July 18, 2014, www.statsamerica.org/innovation/index.html.

23. "Alan Kay Educator and Computing Pioneer," *TED Conferences, LLC*, July 18, 2014, http://www.ted.com/speakers/alan_kay.

24. The ARCHAngel (Akron Regional CHange Angel) Network brings together promising technology companies, investors, mentors, service providers and potential strategic partners in Northeast Ohio. The companies often leverage the region's strengths in health care, alternative energy, information technologies, polymers and other advanced materials.

25. Marcia Pledger, "CEO of Quality Electrodynamics Sees Teamwork As Key to Tech Start-ups Success," *The Plain Dealer* (Cleveland, OH), June 16, 2010.

Contributors

Rebecca Bagley is President and CEO of NorTech, a technology-focused organization that strengthens Northeast Ohio's economic vitality by accelerating the pace of innovation in the region. Under her leadership, NorTech is using its emerging industries expertise to foster an innovation environment that provides companies, research institutions, and individuals of diverse backgrounds with new opportunities for collaboration that create jobs, attract capital, and have long-term, economic impact.

A nationally recognized expert in technology-based economic development, Bagley connects with business leaders, policy makers, and other influencers to raise the visibility of Northeast Ohio's technology assets, position the region as an innovation hub, and attract resources.

Before joining NorTech in 2009, Bagley served as Deputy Secretary for the Technology Investment Office of the Pennsylvania Department of Community and Economic Development (DCED). She previously was Director of the Venture Investment for DCED and has worked for several investment banks, most notably JPMorgan Chase.

Richard J. Batyko has over twenty years of Fortune 100 and non-profit communications, marketing and brand management experience. Currently he is serving as President of the Regional Marketing Alliance of Northeast Ohio. In this role, Batyko is leading corporate, civic, and foundation-backed effort to market the Northeast Ohio region, including Cleveland, Akron, Canton, and Youngstown, to external and internal audiences. Batyko has served as director of Communications for Babcock & Wilcox; as a director of Communications and Brand Management for AlliedSignal, as manager at e-Media and News Management at Honeywell International, and as Vice President for Marketing & Communications at The Cleveland Foundation. He is a graduate of Ohio University's E. W. Scripps School of Journalism, holds his accreditation with the Public Relations Society of America (PRSA) and earned his Master of Public Relations from Kent State University. In 2009, he was inducted into PRSA's prestigious College of Fellows. He has been a speaker at national professional association conferences on topics including media relations, branding, marketing, public relations, and social media. He has been published in the Public Relations Journal and has contributed to academic works and texts, most recently to an ABC-CLIO book on advertising.

Ronald Bucci is currently the Administrative Director of the MetroHealth System in Cleveland, OH. Concurrently, he is adjunct faculty at Walsh University, University of Phoenix, Walden University, and Colorado Technical University. He has just published his first book called *Medicine and Business* from Springer Publishers. He is the previous Interim Vice President of Professional/Support Services and Administrative Director of Radiology at Akron Children's Hospital. Prior experiences were as Director of Imaging at Prexus Health—a health care delivery system based in Cincinnati—President and CEO of QuickClinic and PET of Ohio. He received a Bachelor of Science in Allied Health, Radiologic Technology from The Ohio State University, an MBA from the University of Pittsburgh, and a PhD in Healthcare Administration from Southern California University of Professional Studies. Bucci is currently enrolled in the Six Sigma/Lean Training Program.

Mike Burkons attended Connecticut College and went on to receive a law degree from the Cleveland-Marshall College of Law. While at Connecticut College, the idea for his company came one day when two Catholic nuns were offering a hole-in-one contest at a local golf course. After four months of developing and planning, Burkons produced his hole-in-one technology. Once installed on a golf course, a golfer can purchase a ticket to try his luck at hitting a hole-in-one at a hole with the Charitee Hole-in-One Monitoring System. If the golfer succeeds, he will win $1000 and the course's youth golf efforts will receive $500.

Miko Cakmak is Harold A. Morton Chair and Distinguished Professor of Polymer Engineering at The University of Akron. His area of expertise is on identification, modeling, and simulation of complex structural mechanisms that take place during the course of polymer processing operations of wide range of polymers subjected to solution, melt as well as rubbery state deformation. He also develops novel processes for products in the optics, electronics, and biomaterial device fields. Current activities are focused on real time measurements of true mechano-optical and mechano-electrical properties of polymers undergoing flexing, uni and biaxial deformation for optics and flexible electronics applications. He is actively developing novel processes to address the needs of emerging markets. Towards this goal, his group recently developed a hybrid electrospinning/solution casting multipurpose processing platform to produce functional polymer films including conductive transparent flexible and stretchable films for flexible electronics. Additionally he designed and constructed pilot R2R machine that applies electric, magnetic, thermal fields to orient particles and phases in "Z" direction (normal to the film plane) to produce films for functional applications including separation membranes and wide range of devices. All these near commercial scale machines are located at brand new National Polymer Innovation Center at The University of Akron dedicated to roll-to-roll manufacturing of functional polymer films.

Thomas V. Chema was the President of Hiram College from 2003 to 2014. A native of East Liverpool, Ohio, Chema was a 1968 graduate of the University of Notre Dame and a 1971 Cum Laude graduate of Harvard Law School. He began his career with the Cleveland-based law firm of Arter & Hadden in 1971 and became a partner in 1979. He took a leave of absence in 1983 to serve as Executive Director of the Ohio Lottery Commission. In 1985, he was asked to become Chairman of the Ohio Public Utilities Commission. In 1990, he was appointed Executive Director of the Gateway Economic Development Corporation and was responsible for overseeing the public/private partnership that led to the financing and construction of Progressive Field and Quicken Loans Arena in Cleveland. He then resumed his law practice and in recent years has consulted across the country on sports and entertainment-related economic development projects as President of Gateway Consultants Group, Inc. Chema is recognized as an expert on energy and telecommunications economics and regulation, infrastructure planning, and developing public/private partnerships. He has published numerous articles on these topics and frequently lectures throughout the country, including assignments at the Graduate School of Design at Harvard University.

Shon Christy's passion for driving online buzz combined with almost twenty years of marketing experience,came Christy Creative, Northeast Ohio's first niche, full-service social media marketing agency was born. Clients in the retail, consumer goods, service and health care industries have turned to Christy for his expertise in crafting strategic social media messaging that monetize the web. Christy sold the firm at the end of 2013 and has recently started a new firm, Focal Point Social Media, with his partner Mark Krohn from venture capital company Acquire Investments. Christy's marketing portfolio includes well-known brands such as Bacardi, Jack Daniels, and Buffalo Wild Wings. His work has been featured in *Inside Business*; *Smart Business;* the *Akron Beacon Journal*; and the *Young Professional Roadmap*. Ever the entrepreneur, Christy has launched

Beckett's Buddies, a fundraising group to support those with Down syndrome in honor of his three-year-old son Beckett. Equally passionate about philanthropy as he is about digital marketing and social media, Shon has an impressive track record of community service. He regularly donates a portion of his company revenues to the Upside of Downs, a nonprofit advocacy for individuals with Down syndrome in NE Ohio. A member of The Rotary Club of Akron, Christy serves as the president, and has served as the Chili Open cochairman, PR chairman, and president-elect. Additionally, he serves on the Board of Stand Up for Downs, United Disability Services, The LuMind Foundation (Down syndrome cognition research) and The Rotary Camp for Children with Special Needs. Lastly, Christy is extremely involved in the United Way of Summit County as a member of the Young Leaders Society and the Tocqueville Society where he also serves on the cabinet. Recently, Christy Creative was bestowed with the Greater Akron Small Business Councils Excellence in Business: Emerging Business award, the Distinguished Sales and Marketing Executive Award from SMEI, and is a member of the 31st class of Leadership Akron. In 2012, the Greater Akron Chamber of Commerce Young Professionals Network recognized Christy with the prestigious 30 For the Future award for his community service and business leadership. He is always seeking ways in which to give back to the Akron community and is fully committed to staying current on social media and digital marketing trends.

Christopher Clark is the founder of a Cleveland-based organization, Sunflower Solutions, whose claim to fame is the world's only solar tracker designed for use in remote and developing areas, known as the emPower Plant™. Using this technology, Sunflower—founded in 2009—aims to improve the lives of men, women, and children around the world by helping bring them electricity, acting in terms of his belief that improving solar power will then improve education, health care, clean water, economic growth, and agriculture. Clark, an interdisciplinary Business Management graduate of Miami

University of Ohio, created this technology through a senior capstone project. Today, Sunflower Solutions, founded in 2009, has over a dozen installations in six countries, including Kenya, India, Nigeria, Rwanda, Togo, and the US.

Stavros T. Constantinou is an Associate Professor of Geography at The Ohio State University, Mansfield Campus. His interests include the study of migration and ethnicity from the quantitative point of view. His published research includes two major studies on emigration from Greece to the United States and emigration from Cyprus to the United Kingdom (with Nicholas D. Diamantides) as well as a study of Greek American ethnic identity (with Milton E. Harvey). In addition to survey data, he has used census and church records to examine the changing spatial dimensions of Greek populations in the United States.

Charis Eng is the founding chair of the Genomic Medicine Institute at the Cleveland Clinic, founding director of the institute's clinical component, the Center for Personalized Genetic Healthcare, and Professor and vice chairman of the Department of Genetics and Genome Sciences at Case Western Reserve University School of Medicine. She was honored with the Sondra J. and Stephen R. Hardis Endowed Chair in Cancer Genomic Medicine in 2008 and the American Cancer Society Clinical Research Professorship in 2009. More recently, she was elected to the Institute of Medicine of the US National Academies of Sciences for her achievements and leadership in genetics- and genomics-based research and personalized health care. Eng's research has been acknowledged as the paradigm for performing cancer genetics research which can be brought to clinical practice. At the clinical interface, she is acknowledged as one of the rare "go to" people on what is and how to implement genetic- and genomics-enabled personalized health care.

John M. Finley II is chairman and CEO of MemPro Materials Corporation. He is also managing director of CLEVECAP LLC (an investment banking firm) and chairman of 2Dme Inc (a video communications company). He has been an investor and advisor to entrepreneurs on capital and market development strategies since 1981. He is a graduate of St. Lawrence University with a BS in Physics, the University of Rochester with an MBA, and the Quartermaster School of the US Army from which he holds an honorable discharge. Before founding MemPro, CLEVECAP, and 2Dme, he had a career in corporate finance and was CEO of Oxygen Enrichment Company (medical products) and Membrane Products Corporation (filtration products). He has collaborated with major research universities and national laboratories in product development and technology transfer. Finley was the founding president of the Chief Executives Network for Manufacturing (Albany, NY), vice president and president of the St. Lawrence Alumni Executive Council, trustee of St. Lawrence University, volunteer for the Snowboard Outreach Society and the Alpenglow Chamber Music Festival.

Thomas A. Finnerty is the Associate Director of the Center for Urban and Regional Studies at Youngstown State University. Finnerty earned his BA in Geography from Youngstown State University and his MA in Geography from The University of Akron. He is an adjunct faculty member at YSU. While at the Center, he has directed and participated in numerous grant projects, planning exercises, feasibility studies, and other projects for the city of Youngstown and other local governments throughout the Mahoning Valley region.

Hiroyuki Fujita, a Japanese national who came to Cleveland in 1992 to attend Case Western Reserve University (CWRU), is founder, president and CEO of Quality Electrodynamics (QED), a company in Mayfield Village that manufactures and sells state-of-the-art MRI coils worldwide. In 2009, *Forbes* magazine designated QED as one of the 20 Most Promising Companies in America. In 2010 and 2011, *Inc. Magazine* named Fujita as one of the top entrepreneurs in America and placed QED in the *Inc* 500, calling it one of America's fastest growing companies. Also in 2010, Fujita won the Ernst & Young Entrepreneur of the Year Award Northeast Ohio in the category of Industry Manufacturing. In recognition of growing a successful high-tech manufacturing company and creating high-tech, advanced manufacturing jobs in the health care sector in the United States of America, President Barack Obama and First Lady Michelle Obama invited Fujita to be an honored guest at the 2012 State of the Union Address, and to sit in the First Lady's Box.. Today, Fujita is an Adjunct Professor of Physics, Radiology and Electrical Engineering at CWRU and at The University of Queensland, Australia. In 2013, Fujita was named one of the twenty-six US Manufacturing Council members, advising the US Secretary of Commerce, and serves on various boards. He holds sixteen patents and has published more than thirty papers and abstracts in respected engineering, imaging and physics journals. Fujita has received numerous awards from state, national, and international governments for his excellence in imaging technology and manufacturing, including the 2013 Presidential award for export, E-Award, from the US Department of Commerce. Nikkei Business named Fujita as one of the most influential 100 people for Japan in 2014.

Kathryn Wertheim Hexter directs the Center for Community Planning and Development, Maxine Goodman Levin College of Urban Affairs, Cleveland State University. She joined the Levin College in 1986. A planner and public policy analyst, Hexter has over twenty-five years of experience managing and directing projects and evaluating programs in the areas of community development, housing, mortgage foreclosure, neighborhood development, sustainable development, low-income energy assistance, city and regional planning, and civic engagement. She has worked extensively with federal, state, and local governmental, philanthropic and nonprofit organizations. She recently completed a study "Revitalizing Distressed, Older Suburbs" for the What Works Collaborative of the Urban Institute http://www.urban.org/what-works-collaborative.cfm. She is the founding director of the Levin College Forum Program, a community engagement and education program, recognized by *Northern Ohio Live* (2005) as "a springboard for economic and social progress throughout the region." Hexter holds a master's degree in City and Regional Planning from Harvard University. Prior to joining the College she worked in community and governmental relations for the East Ohio Gas Company and as a planning consultant.

Deborah D. Hoover has served since 2007 as president and CEO of The Burton D. Morgan Foundation, a private foundation dedicated to fostering entrepreneurship in Northeast Ohio.. Hoover was instrumental in establishing the Foundation's Northeast Ohio Collegiate Entrepreneurship Program, a Kauffman CampusesSM Initiative, to spread entrepreneurship across liberal arts campuses; and in bringing the Blackstone LaunchPad Program to the Northeast Ohio region in partnership with The Blackstone Charitable Foundation. She serves as chair of the Fund for Our Economic Future, a philanthropic collaborative created in 2004 to advance the economic competitiveness of Northeast Ohio. In April, 2014 she was elected to the Board of The Foundation Center, the leading source of information about philanthropy worldwide. Hoover serves on the Board of Trustees of Western Reserve Academy and is a member of the National Council for The Norman Rockwell Museum in Stockbridge, Massachusetts. Hoover earned her BA from Williams College and a Masters in the History of Art from the University of Chicago. She continued graduate studies at George Washington University National Law Center where she earned a JD degree and was a member of the Law Review. She is a member of the bar in the District of Columbia, New Hampshire, and Ohio.

Marjorie Carlson Hurst has had an interesting and varied career. It began in 1974, when she was hired by Ohio Bell Telephone Company as Ohio's second female lineman. She went on to spend twenty-five years with AT&T in sales and marketing management. In 2000, Carlson Hurst transitioned to a second career in academics. She is the Dean of the School of Business & Leadership at Malone University. She has been responsible for launching new programs, improving quality, and major accreditation efforts. She encourages staff, students, and faculty to grow to their maximum potential and see beyond the obvious. Carlson Hurst has a BA from Malone University, an EMBA from Baldwin Wallace College, and a doctorate in Business Administration from Nova Southeastern University in Fort Lauderdale.

Damir Janigro is a Professor of Molecular Medicine and Director of Cerebrovascular research at the Cleveland Clinic. He was born in Croatia but received most of his higher education in Milan, Italy where he obtained a PhD in Physiology and Biophysics in 1982. After postdoctoral training at Karolinska in Stockholm and at the University of Washington in Seattle, he became Assistant Professor of Neurological Surgery in 1989. He remained at the University of Washington as Associate Professor until 1999. Janigro has served as chairman for the Brain 1 study sections of the American Heart Association, as chair of the Department of Defense Epilepsy panel, and has been a permanent member of two NIH reviewing panels. He received numerous multiyear NIH grants which led to the discovery of patented technologies in the field of blood-brain barrier research. He has also received funding from the Department of Energy and private companies in the US and abroad. He is the cofounder of Flocel, Inc., a NEO start-up company, and holds numerous patents related to biomedical diagnostics.

Mitchell Kahan is director emeritus of the Akron Art Museum, where he was director and CEO from 1986 to 2013. He holds a PhD in Art History from City University of New York Graduate School, and bachelor's and master's degrees from University of Virginia and Columbia University, where he studied architectural history and art history. Since the 1970s, Kahan has written and lectured extensively on twentieth century American art, including the history of corporate collecting, folk art, art of the 1930s, and contemporary art. He has been awarded fellowships from the Smithsonian Institution and the National Endowment for the Arts and has served on advisory panels for local, state, and federal arts agencies. In 1984, he was a guest curator for the Louisiana World's Fair. He is a past president of Akron Roundtable, Akron Area Arts Alliance and Ohio's Intermuseum Conservation Association and is a former trustee of the Association of Art Museum Directors, an organization representing Canada, Mexico, and the United States. He is the coauthor of a book on the collection of the Akron Art Museum and was honored with the Distinguished Museum Professional Award for 2003 by the Ohio Museums Association. In 2008, he was granted the Robert P. Bergman Award from the Cleveland Arts Prize and the Nonprofit Leadership Award from Case Western Reserve University's Mandel School for Nonprofit Management.

Joseph Kennedy's contributions to rubber science and technology are vast, particularly in the fields of carbocationic polymerizations, rubbery biomaterials, and macromolecular design and engineering. Kennedy received the equivalent of a BS in Chemistry from the University of Budapest in Hungary in 1948, earned his PhD in Biochemistry at the University of Vienna in Austria in 1954, and an MBA from Rutgers University in 1961. He was a postdoc at McGill University and at the Sorbonne. He came to The University of Akron in 1970, playing a fundamental role in the development of the College of Polymer Science & Polymer Engineering, now ranked as the #2 graduate academic program in Polymer Science in the nation. Kennedy is author to four books, over seven hundred refereed publications in top journals, and has over one hundred issued US patents. Some of his awards include two American Chemical Society Awards, one in Polymer Chemistry (1985) and one in Applied Polymer Science (1995), and the Rubber Division's George S. Whitby Award in 1996 for excellence in teaching and research, the Goodyear Medal (2008), Fellow of the American Chemical Society (2010), Charter Fellow of National Academy of Inventors (2013), Honorary Doctorates from the University of Budapest, and The University of Akron. Kennedy has trained more than one hundred fifty students and postdoctorals who became successful industrial leaders or professors internationally. His mentorship is unparalleled. Currently in his 80s, he is still active and in his office every day inventing/developing new rubbers.

Norman Krumholz is a professor in the Levin College of Urban Affairs at Cleveland State University. He is a past president of both the American Planning Association (APA) and the American Institute of Certified Planners (AICP). Prior to his joining the faculty at CSU, Krumholz served as planning director of Cleveland for ten years. Krumholz has written or edited five books on planning and urban neighborhoods and has published in many professional journals. His book *Making Equity Planning Work*, with Professor John Forester, won the Paul Davidoff award for best progressive book of the year from the Associated Collegiate Schools of Planning. Krumholz's equity planning practice in behalf of the poor and working class people of Cleveland has become a national model for planners in other large cities who are struggling to retain their industrial and economic base while making their neighborhoods more livable.

John Lauletta is CEO/CTO of Exacter, Inc., and has been involved in electric utility measurement technology since 1975. Lauletta's career includes ten years with American Electric Power as Measurements Manager, fourteen years as VP at Scientific Columbus and most recently as CEO/CTO of Exacter, Inc. Lauetta holds engineering degrees from The Ohio State University and Purdue University and is the past chair of the Central Ohio Power Engineering Society Chapter of IEEE. Lauetta has several patents in predictive failure technologies. Exacter, Inc. is a developer of predictive technologies for electric utility reliability, grid conditions-based assessment, and preventive maintenance.

Thomas A. Maraffa received his bachelor's, master's, and PhD degrees in Geography from The Ohio State University. He recently retired as a faculty member at Youngstown State University where he served since 1985. Between 1980 and 1985 he was an assistant professor of geography at Virginia Tech. His research and teaching interests have been in economic geography particularly transportation and commuting. He has been active in geographic education and currently serves as cocoordinator of the Ohio Geographic Alliance. While at Youngstown State, Maraffa served as chairperson of the department of geography from 1992 to 2002 and in the chief of staff role in the Office of the President between 2002 and 2010.

Michael Mariola has had a lifelong interest in great food, beginning at the earliest of ages with the hearty home-style cooking of his French mother. He started in the restaurant business at the age of fourteen, first working in the kitchen of The College of Wooster, then, after graduating high school, at Ray's Place in Kent, Ohio. He returned to Wooster for a position in the kitchen at The Wooster Inn, and, from there, was hired as a prep cook by renowned chef Parker Bosley, of Parker's Restaurant and Bistro Bar in Cleveland. Within six months, Mariola was promoted to Sous Chef, running the kitchen. During his time, he was also encouraged to serve internships under the esteemed French chefs Christian Constant at Le Violon d'Ingres in Paris and Michael Richard at Citronelle in Washington, DC. In July 2002, Mariola opened the South Market Bistro in downtown Wooster, and in September 2008, opened the Square Steakhouse. In the summer of 2011, Mariola opened a gourmet burger bar called The Rail, located at Summit Mall in Akron, OH. In addition to his restaurant building and operating experience, he has also neared completion of the renovation of the historic downtown Wooster Gold Star Building: a sixteen thousand square foot building that houses The South Market Bistro, Spoon Market and Butcher, offices, and newly constructed loft apartments. Mariola is an active member of the Wooster community, currently serving on the Main Street Wooster Board of Directors as well as the College of Wooster Center for Entrepreneurial Studies Board. He lives in Wooster along with his wife and four children.

Steven Marks and partner, Harvey Nelson, founded Main Street Muffins (now Main Street Gourmet) in 1987, and since then, were chosen by *Inc. Magazine* and Ernst & Young as the 1993 Entrepreneurs of the Year Award for Northeastern Ohio. Senator John Glenn selected Marks as his sole choice to be a delegate for the 1995 White House Conference on Small Business. In 1994 and 2011 the US Small Business Administration selected the partners as the Small Business Person(s) of the Year. The University of Akron has also recognized Marks with the 1999 Simonetti Distinguished Business Alumni Award, the 2000 Outstanding Beta Alpha Psi Alumnus Award and the 2006 University of Akron Alumni Honor Award. Steve is also the founder of the Akron Marathon, launched in 2003 by a family foundation he started. In 2005, the Akron Marathon was recognized as one of the 50 Greatest US Marathons. Main Street Gourmet founded an award-winning program with Akron General Medical Center called Muffins for Mammograms, designed to raise money for women who cannot afford breast cancer screening costs. To date, the program has raised more than $250,000. Community involvement currently includes participating as a board of trustee member for the Greater Akron Chamber and chairman of The Akron Marathon Charitable Corp.

D. Kirk Neiswander is the Founder and President of The Entrepreneurs EDGE, a nonprofit organization founded in 2005 that focuses on innovation, entrepreneurship, economic development, and midmarket companies—all in Northeast Ohio. Before taking part in this business endeavor, he was an officer of Enterprise Development, Inc., and had a more than twenty-two-year career at Case Western Reserve University, where he created many new courses, conferences, retreats, breakfast series, recognition events, networking events, and specialized services for midmarket companies. He has an MBA from the Weatherhead School of Management at Case Western Reserve University in General Management, and a BA from Denison University in Mathematics/Economics.

George R. Newkome received his BS and PhD in Chemistry from Kent State University and was a postdoctoral fellow at Princeton University before joining Louisiana State University where he became a full professor in 1978, and LSU Distinguished Research Master in 1982. In 1986, Newkome joined the University of South Florida as their first Vice President for Research with a faculty appointment in chemistry and was named Distinguished Research Professor in 1992. In 2001, he became Vice President for Research and Dean, Graduate School at The University of Akron, the Oelschlager Professor of Science and Technology, and professor in the departments of Polymer Science and Chemistry. He is the President and CEO of the University of Akron Research Foundation as well as a Fellow in the AAAS, Royal Society of Chemistry, and National Academy of Inventors. He has published over 470 papers, sixty issued patents, and edited/written over twenty scientific books and monographs.

Luis Proenza was the president of The University of Akron from 1998 to 2014. During his tenure, the University financed $620 million in capital construction to completely transform its campus, adding twenty-one new facilities, eighteen major renovations and additions and thirty-four acres of new green space, thereby becoming one of the most attractive metropolitan campuses in the nation. Proenza also led community efforts to create two key enterprises: a University Park Alliance that is revitalizing a fifty-block area surrounding its campus, and the $200 million Austen BioInnovation Institute in Akron, a partnership with three area hospitals and a medical school to establish Akron as a center for biomaterials and biomedicine. These and other initiatives have distinguished the University nationally and internationally and have made UA a recognized national model for technology commercialization, economic development, and corporate and community partnerships.

In 2001, President George W. Bush named Proenza to the President's Council of Advisors on Science and Technology, the nation's highest-level policy advisory group for science and technology.

Proenza cochaired PCAST's committee on Public-Private Partnerships and worked on panels on US Research and Development Investments, Technology Transfer, Alternative Energy, Energy Efficiency and Advanced Manufacturing, Personalized Medicine, Information Technology, and Nanotechnology. In 2004, the Secretary of Energy appointed him chairman of the Science and Mathematics Education Task Force and, later, to the Secretary of Energy Advisory Board.

Proenza earned his BA from Emory University (1965), his MA from The Ohio State University (1966), and PhD from the University of Minnesota (1971).

Judit E. Puskas received a PhD in plastics and rubber technology in 1985, and an MESc in organic and biochemical engineering in 1977, from the Technical University of Budapest, Hungary. She started her academic career in 1996, and has since been published in more than 370 publications, including technical reports. She is an inventor or coinventor of thirty-one US patents and applications. She has been awarded seven NSF grants, including a Phase II SBIR and an AIR award in this year totaling $1.5 million. She received her first NIH grant (the first ever in the Department of Polymer Science) in 2010. She is the recipient of several other awards, including the 1999 Professional Engineers of Ontario, the Canada Medal in Research and Development, a 2000 Premier's Research Excellence Award, the 2004 Mercator Professorship Award from the Deutschen Forschungsgemeinschaft, German Research Foundation, the LANXESS (previously Bayer) Industrial Chair 1998–2008, the 2009 Chemistry of Thermoplastic Elastomers Award of the Rubber Division of the American Chemical Society, the Woman of Achievement Award and the 2014 UA Outstanding Researcher Award. She was elected Fellow of the American Institute of Medical and Biological Engineering in 2010, and Fellow of IUPAC in 2013. As a coinventor of the polymer used on the Taxus® coronary stent, Puskas helped The University of Akron generate more than $5 million in license fees. Puskas and her business partners have founded spin-off companies to market some of her new polymers. She was named the Joseph M. Gingo Chair in Chemical Engineering in June 2014.

Majid Rashidi received his PhD in 1983 and BSME in 1981 from Case Western Reserve University. Following his graduation in 1986, Rashidi worked at NASA for the Institute of Computational Mechanic in Propulsion. In fall of 1987, he started a tenure-track position in the Mechanical Engineering Department at Cleveland State University, and was promoted to the rank of Professor in 2008. Additionally, Rashidi has twenty-four years of machine design experience related to real-world engineering problem solving for industry, where his research work has resulted in several publications in refereed technical journals as well as six patents in print. Rashidi's latest patent has been reduced to a fully functional wind harnessing system that is installed on the rooftop of the Plant Service Building at Cleveland State University. This innovative wind harnessing system has been featured in many national and international journals, including *New York Times*, *Business Week*, *Reuters*, and *Wind Tech-International.*

Neil Reid is Professor of Geography and Planning and director of the Urban Affairs Center at the University of Toledo. He is an industrial geographer with research interests in the theory and application of industrial clusters. He currently serves as chair of the International Geographical Union's Commission on the Dynamics of Economic Spaces and as executive director of the North American Regional Science Council.

Bernard Sater and **Neil Sater** are the father and son founders of GreenField Solar. Bernard is the inventor and is primarily a skilled technologist, rather than a businessman. Neil is more focused on the business side of their entrepreneurial venture.

Bernard Sater had a long and successful career at NASA Lewis Research Center (now named Glenn Research Center) with broad experience in engineering. His most recent position was Project Manager for Advanced Development, where he was responsible for the International Space Station solar cells and associated materials. He retired early in 1994 to devote his time to commercializing his unique PhotoVolt™ solar cell invention. Bernard holds a BEE degree from The Ohio State University and an MSEE from Cleveland State University, with additional graduate studies at the University of Toledo. Bernard has been awarded five patents.

Neil Sater left Intel Corp. at the beginning of 2008 to devote full time to GreenField. At Intel he managed America's Comms, Media, and Software business development teams, driving commercial success of the company's new products and major growth initiatives such as WiMAX, Centrino and Atom Processors. Prior to Intel, Neil worked as an engineer and engineering manager for Spectra-Physics, where he was an Associate Scientific Fellow. Neil taught in the Myers University MBA program from 2000–2002, and holds one patent with others pending. He holds a BSEE from The Ohio State and an MBA in finance/marketing from Wright State University.

Bruce W. Smith is a Professor Emeritus of Geography at Bowling Green State University, and a Research Fellow in BGSU's Center for Regional Development. He also has been a Visiting Research Fellow in the Urban Affairs Center at the University of Toledo. He is an industrial geographer whose recent research has focused on cluster-based economic development, with an emphasis on the greenhouse industry of northwest Ohio. He is particularly interested in the application of social network analysis to understanding the functioning of clusters.

Bahman Taheri is the CEO of AlphaMicron (AMI™), a Kent-based research and development company founded in 1996 initially designed for the Department of Defense. The company's initial focus was to create an electronically controllable tint technology for US Air Force fighter pilots. In the process, it created the world's only liquid crystal visor that provides electronic tint on demand. This product has since been commercialized in products such as ski goggles, autodimming automotive mirrors, and energy-efficient adaptive windows. Recent accolades include Innovation of the Month from *Motorcycle Consumer News*, and a Manny Award for excellence in manufacturing in the product development category.

Andrew Vaeth is the CEO & Cofounder of Cureo. He is a respected pioneer in web services and on-demand technologies, and has guided his organizations to market success with multiple world-class workforce software solutions. Prior to his role at Cureo, he cofounded and served as president and chief executive officer of ExpenseWire, which achieved significant recognition as a high growth, emerging leader in the expense management software space before it was purchased in a positive transaction. ExpenseWire is now a unit of Paychex (NASDAQ: PAYX). Learn more about his current internet software project at Cureo.com. Born in Cleveland Heights, Ohio, raised in Wooster, Ohio, he is a graduate of Indiana University (Bloomington). Andrew currently resides in Wooster, Ohio, with his wife and two children.

Russ Vernon is the retired chairman of West Point Market, an upscale family-owned specialty food store in Akron, Ohio. Founded in 1936 by his father and two business partners, the store has become a regional destination for professional chefs, recreational cooks, and people who love good food. In addition to other publications, West Point Market has been featured in the *Wall Street Journal, New York Times, Bon Appetite, Food & Wine Magazine, Esquire, Nation's Business, Inc Magazine,* and *Reader's Digest*. ABC's Good Morning America featured West Point Market in a national segment on businesses acclaimed for their high levels of customer service. He is a recipient of the 2014 Specialty Food Association Lifetime Achievement Award.

Vernon was named Small Business Person of the Year by the Small Business Administration, Entrepreneur of the Year by the Akron Regional Development Board, and Sales and Marketing Executive of the Year by the Akron Sales & Marketing Association. In 1995 he was an Ohio delegate representing small business to the

White House. Vernon is past chairman of the Fitzgerald Institute of Entrepreneurial Studies at The University of Akron. He was an Ernst & Young Entrepreneur Finalist and inducted into the Family Business Hall of Fame at Case Western University's Weatherhead School of Business. Vernon volunteers time as a counselor for SCORE, America's counselors to small business, past board member of Goodwill Industries and serves on the Advisory Board for the Hattie Larlham Foundation. He authored the *West Point Market Cookbook* published by The University of Akron Press. Russ has three sons and resides with his wife, Peg, at their home in Akron, Ohio.

Lauren Wolf is the Founder and CEO of Aeroclay, a 2009 technology transfer company commercializing a patented platform technology called aerogel, under an exclusive licensing agreement with Case Western Reserve University. Prior to that, Wolf was a founding member and C-level executive of DLM Diversified LLC, and a partner with Deloitte from 1985 to 2002. Wolf received a BBA in Accounting from The Max M. Fisher College of Business at The Ohio State University, and a BBA in Business Administration-Accounting from Cleveland State University. She was given the Gold Medal and Elijah Watt Sells Award for high performance on the CPA exam, was named Woman of Achievement by the YWCA, is a founding board member for Dress for Success Cleveland, and a former board chair for the same organization.